"In all the world there is no kind of framework within which we find consciousness in the plural. This is simply something we construct because of the temporal plurality of individuals. But it is a false construction...the only solution to this conflict, in so far as any is available to us at all, lies in the ancient wisdom of the Upanishads."

— Erwin Schrödinger

"When I read the Bhagavad Gita and reflect about how God created this universe, everything else seems so superfluous."

— Albert Einstein

"Mankind's origins can be traced to India, where the human mind got the first shapes of wisdom and virtue with a simplicity, strength and sublimity which has — frankly spoken — nothing, nothing at all equivalent in our philosophical, European world."

— Johann Gottfried von Herder

"When we read the poetical and philosophical monuments of the East — above all, those of India, which are beginning to spread in Europe — we discover there...truths so profound, that we are constrained to bend the knee before the philosophy of the East, and to see in this cradle of the human race the native land of the highest philosophy."

— Victor Cousin

"The marvel of the Bhagavad-Gita is its truly beautiful revelation of life's wisdom which enables philosophy to blossom into religion."

— Hermann Hesse

"If I were asked under what sky the human mind has most fully developed some of its choicest gifts, has most deeply pondered over the greatest problems of life, and has found solutions of some of them which well deserve the attention even of those who have studied Plato and Kant, I should point to India. And if I were to ask myself from what literature we who have been nurtured almost exclusively on the thoughts of Greeks and Romans, and of the Semitic race, may draw the corrective which is most wanted in order to make our inner life more perfect, more comprehensive, more universal, in fact more truly human a life…again I should point to India."

— MAX MÜLLER

"The Bhagavad-Gita is the most systematic statement of spiritual evolution of endowing value to mankind. It is one of the most clear and comprehensive summaries of perennial philosophy ever revealed; hence its enduring value is subject not only to India but to all of humanity."

— ALDOUS HUXLEY

"The apparent multiplication of gods is bewildering at the first glance, but you soon discover that they are the same GOD. There is always one uttermost God who defies personification. This makes Hinduism the most tolerant religion in the world, because its one transcendent God includes all possible gods."

— GEORGE BERNARD SHAW

"The Bhagavad Gita…is the most beautiful philosophical song existing in any known tongue."

— ROBERT OPPENHEIMER

"Our most valuable and most instructive materials in the history of man are treasured up in India."

— MARK TWAIN

SACRED JEWELS
OF YOGA

SACRED JEWELS OF YOGA

WISDOM FROM INDIA'S BELOVED SCRIPTURES, TEACHERS, MASTERS, AND MONKS

COMPILED AND EDITED BY DAVE DELUCA

New World Library
Novato, California

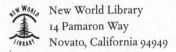
New World Library
14 Pamaron Way
Novato, California 94949

An earlier version of this book was published under the title *Spiritual Jewels*.

Text design by Tona Pearce Myers

Library of Congress Cataloging-in-Publication Data
Sacred jewels of yoga : wisdom from India's beloved scriptures, teachers, masters, and monks / compiled and edited by Dave DeLuca.
     p.   cm.
"An earlier version of this book was previously published under the title Spiritual jewels."
Includes bibliographical references.
ISBN 978-1-60868-040-5 (pbk. : alk. paper)
1. Yoga. 2. Sacred books—Yoga. 3. India—Religion. 4. Philosophy, Indic. 5. Hindu philosophy. I. DeLuca, Dave.
B132.Y6S313 2011
181'.45—dc23   2011019874

First printing, August 2011
ISBN 978-1-60868-040-5
Printed in Canada on 100% postconsumer-waste recycled paper

g New World Library is a proud member of the Green Press Initiative.

10 9 8 7 6 5 4 3 2 1

Dedicated to Swami Vivekananda,
and his mission of bringing
the sacred yoga wisdom
of Vedanta to the world

Those who deny the Lord deny themselves;
Those who affirm the Lord affirm themselves.
The wise, not the unwise, realize the Lord.

— TAITTIRIYA UPANISHAD

CONTENTS

THE BHAGAVAD GITA

Astavakra Samhita

Patanjali's Yoga Sutras

Narada's Bhakti Sutras

Srimad Bhagavatam

DHAMMAPADA

SARVEPALLI RADHAKRISHNAN

SWAMI VIVEKANANDA

INTRODUCTION

This anthology is meant to give lovers of yoga a reference book in which they will be able to easily find cherished passages from some of the most revered yoga scriptures and commentary in India's history. Because *yoga* is one of the oldest living religious words, and because over the millennia it has had so many different and even contradictory meanings, I wanted to present yoga's most important source scriptures and teachings in the clearest and most accessible way possible: in one-page passages where readers can experience for themselves the original and highest intent for the word, the wisdom, and the practices of yoga.

For thousands of years yoga teachers have taught the scriptures one passage at a time, having their students study and meditate on each passage for hours, even days at a time before moving on to the next. This is a time-tested process that has consistently cultivated great spiritual progress throughout history, allowing for the deepest meanings of the wisdom to take root in the hearts and minds of earnest aspirants.

In our modern world this seems too painstaking and even detrimental a process. Most of us just want to get through whatever material is before us — let's just read it, learn it, and be done with it. But this approach is antithetical to the tradition and practice of yoga. Yoga is meant to be thoughtful and contemplative, yet active and even scientific in its conscious and methodical approach to spiritual growth.

I have compiled this book so that the reader may open to any page at any time, and, with ease, be introduced to a yoga passage of great historical and spiritual significance. I can certainly attest to the power of these passages in my own life. I will never forget when I was first introduced to many of them. I remember reading them over and over again, my whole being on fire in a constant and overwhelming experience of awe, reverence, and gratitude for the glorious insights and revelations they were bringing into my life. At the time I had no idea how many people throughout history had experienced the same exquisite feelings that these scriptures were evoking in me. My most powerful recognition of the enormous love that others have felt for these spiritual treasures came when I first read Ralph Waldo Emerson's description of the Bhagavad Gita. Having been raised Unitarian, as Emerson was, I knew him to be one of the most brilliant and eloquent philosophers that America had ever produced, and so his words of praise were extraordinarily powerful to me. I will never forget the tears of joy and recognition I experienced when I first read these words: "I owed a magnificent day to the Bhagavad Gita. It was the first of books; it was as if an empire spoke to us, nothing small or unworthy, but large, serene, consistent, the voice of an old intelligence which in another age and climate had pondered and thus disposed of the same questions which exercise us.... Let us cherish this venerable oracle."

This is exactly how I have felt since the first day I was exposed to India's great yoga scriptures and teachers, and for this I will be forever grateful. It is in the spirit of my deepest gratitude for these spiritual treasures that I offer them to you in this anthology.

THE UPANISHADS

The word *yoga* comes from the root word *yuj*, meaning to "yoke" or "unite." The earliest yoga teachings are found in the Upanishads, which are the final portions of the Vedas, India's most ancient and venerated scriptures. The Upanishads contain the oldest extant teachings of the spiritual wisdom, ideals, and practices of yoga: the Oneness of existence, the divinity of each human soul, meditation, karma, rebirth, maya, spiritual psychology, Self-realization, and so on.

The wisdom of the Upanishads is known as the *Vedanta*, meaning the culmination of the Vedas. The Upanishads are the ecstatic expressions of unknown sages who lived thousands of years ago regarding the nature of reality and our relationship to that reality, and they contain the first teachings of the various spiritual disciplines and practices that would come to define the four main mystical yoga pathways in future scriptures.

There have been many subdefinitions of the word *yoga* in the thousands of years of its teachings and practice, with many modern Western definitions reducing its meaning to a series of physical postures, or asanas, but the oldest, truest, and highest meaning of *yoga* is the union of our spirit with the Infinite Spirit, and the many paths and practices that lead to that union. Swami Nikhilananda put it beautifully: "The word 'yoga' denotes the union of individual soul with Universal Soul, and also the means to such union. Hence yoga is the goal of all religions and the basis of all religious practices."

The Upanishads contain the original seeds of all the yoga wisdom from which the vast library of yoga practices would subsequently be fashioned and perfected by countless generations of anonymous spiritual masters devoted to these incredible wisdom pathways.

The first of the great Upanishadic revelations is that the true nature of reality is Oneness. The Upanishads call the Eternal Oneness *Brahman*, the "great breath" or "expanse." Everything in the universe is a temporary expression of the One: everything comes from the One, has its being in the One, and returns to the One. There is nothing in the universe that is not a manifestation of Brahman. According to the *Taittiriya Upanishad*,

> He who has no form assumed many forms;
> He who is infinite appeared finite;
> He who is everywhere assumed a place;
> He who is all wisdom caused ignorance;
> He who is real caused unreality.
>
> It is He who has become everything.
> It is He who gives reality to all.
> Before the universe was created,
> Brahman existed as unmanifest.

This is not mere pantheism, which equates God with nature. According to the Upanishadic seers, even the vast, unimaginable expanse of the known physical universe is absolutely insignificant in scope when compared to the totality of Existence that is Brahman. As the *Isha Upanishad* proclaims,

> Filled with Brahman are the things we see,
> Filled with Brahman are the things we see not,
> From out of Brahman floweth all that is:
> From Brahman all
> Yet He remains the same.

The next monumental revelation of the Upanishads is of the divinity of each human soul. The Upanishads teach that the true essence of each human being is the *Atman*, the sacred Self,

Brahman indwelling. Atman *is* Brahman, Brahman within, and this is the reality of who we are. We are not our bodies, we are not our minds, we are not our thoughts, we are not our ego. We have a body, we have a mind, we have thoughts, and we have an ego, but our highest truth is the Ever-Blessed Atman, the fountainhead of all joy and light and love that is the core and fundamental truth of our being.

One of the most beloved spiritual affirmations, or *mahavakyas*, of the Upanishads is "Tat Tvam Asi," "Thou Art That." It is the supreme teaching that each of us is actually the Divinity in expression, and it is beautifully expressed in the *Chandogya Upanishad* by Uddalaka as he teaches his son Shvetaketu about his and about our relationship with the Infinite:

> "In the beginning was only Being,
> One without a second.
> Out of Himself He brought forth the cosmos,
> and entered into everything in it.
> There is nothing that does not come from Him.
> Of everything He is the inmost Self.
> He is the truth; He is the Self supreme.
> You are that, Shvetaketu; you are that."

The next great spiritual teaching of the Upanishads is that the highest purpose of life is realizing and manifesting the Divinity within us, uniting with It and allowing It to flow unhindered through us in all Its glory. As the *Brihadaranyaka Upanishad* so eloquently expresses, union with Brahman is the supreme goal and the supreme treasure of life:

> Where there is unity,
> One without a second,
> That is the world of Brahman.

This is the supreme goal of life,
The supreme treasure,
the supreme joy.
Those who do not seek this Supreme goal
Live on but a fraction of this joy.

The scriptures teach us that not only is it our sacred duty, our *dharma*, to uphold the highest in us, but it is the *only* way to abiding joy and peace. They tell us that by dedicating ourselves to the sacred goal of uniting with the highest within us, we will eventually reach the goal, the bliss of union with the Supreme Soul.

The next Upanishadic revelations concern the human condition: the makeup of the soul, the causes of our mental and emotional pain, and the impediments that keep us from living in the light and love of the Atman. These teachings form the foundations of the oldest living spiritual psychology. Eloquently, powerfully, and yet with easy-to-understand terminology, the Upanishads teach us how moment to moment there are two modes of knowing through which we can choose to experience life: through the sacred Self, the very truth of our being, where we experience ourselves and the world through wholeness, love, and joy, or through the individualized and unaware ego, where we experience ourselves and the world through the painful illusions of separation, lack, and need. From the *Mundaka Upanishad*:

Like two golden birds
perched on the selfsame tree,
intimate friends,
the ego and the Self dwell in the same body.

The former eats the sweet and sour fruits
of the tree of life,
while the latter looks on in detachment.

As long as we think we are the ego,
we feel attached and fall into sorrow.
But realize that you are the Self,
the Lord of life,
and you will be freed from sorrow.

When you realize that you are the Self,
supreme source of light,
supreme source of love,
you transcend the duality of life
and enter into the unitive state.

The Upanishads teach us that as long as we remain identified with the separate ego, we remain attached to its constant parade of like and dislike, happy and sad, and all its selfish demands, fears, and cravings. The futile struggle of the individual self to experience wholeness through external gratifications will continue as long as we remain ignorant of our Divine Nature and Its inexhaustible joy. According to the *Shvetashvatara Upanishad*:

On this ever-revolving wheel of being
the individual self goes round and round,
through life after life,
believing itself to be a separate creature,
until it sees its identity with the Lord of Love
and attains immortality in the indivisible whole.

Until we come to know the abiding joy of the Atman, we will continue to suffer in ego's false experience of isolation and the fear it perpetuates, oblivious to who we truly are and what is actually causing our neediness and dissatisfactions. And this is nowhere more profoundly illustrated than in the famous chariot analogy of the *Katha Upanishad*:

Know the Self as lord of the chariot,
the body as the chariot itself,
the discriminating intellect as charioteer,
and the mind as reins.
The senses, say the wise, are the horses;
selfish desires are the roads they travel.
When the Self is confused
with the body, mind, and senses,
they point out, He seems
to enjoy pleasure and suffer sorrow.

When one lacks discrimination
and his mind is undisciplined, the senses
run hither and thither like wild horses.
But they obey the rein like trained horses
when one has discrimination
and has made the mind one-pointed.

Those who lack discrimination,
with little control over their thoughts
and far from pure,
reach not the pure state of immortality
but wander from death to death;
but those who have discrimination,
with a still mind and a pure heart,

reach the journey's end,
never again to fall into the jaws of death.

With a discriminating intellect as charioteer
and a trained mind as reins,
they attain the supreme goal of life,
to be united with the Lord of Love.

While the Self is the absolute lord of the chariot, it dwells quietly within the lotus of our heart, detached from the drama of our lives. It does not force itself on us, but waits for us to grow weary of the chase for happiness outside ourselves. As long as we continue to give the selfish desires and sense cravings of the separate ego the power to choose our destinations in life, we will be forced to travel roads that lead to an ever-increasing bondage to the lower in us and an ever-increasing isolation from the highest in us. Until we wake up to our condition and slavery and take a stand, the lower urges will continue to use us for their own selfish ends and, in doing so, will keep us from uniting in purpose with the Atman. Yoga is the great spiritual struggle against the lower and for the higher, and that battle within each of us that must be fought in order to unite with Atman has never been more powerfully portrayed than in the Bhagavad Gita, the most beloved yoga scripture in the world.

The Bhagavad Gita

For thousands of years the Bhagavad Gita, or the Song of God, has been revered for its spiritual power, beauty, clarity, and catholicity. Although not technically an Upanishad, it carries on the Upanishadic tradition in philosophy and form, taking the great and uncodified revelations of yoga wisdom and practice first offered in the Upanishads and fashioning them into a masterwork on spiritual growth. As with the Upanishads, the fundamental philosophical stance of the Gita is that all existence is a manifestation of God, that God exists in all beings as their innermost Self, that the knowledge of and union with the Self, or yoga, is the supreme goal of life, and that ignorance of our Divinity is the true cause of our suffering.

The teachings of the Gita are presented in the form of a dialogue between Sri Krishna and Arjuna on the battlefield of Kurukshetra. The background story of the Gita is important because it forms the basis of an exquisite allegory on the human condition and the internal struggle to unite with Spirit that most profoundly encapsulates the power and the glory of yoga philosophy and practice.

Facing each other on the battlefield of Kurukshetra are two families of royal cousins, the Pandavas and the Kauravas, the sons of Pandu and Dhritarashtra, respectively. Arjuna is one of the Pandava brothers. Because Dhritarashtra was born blind, his younger brother Pandu inherited the ancestral kingdom from their father. Pandu died young, so the five young Pandavas, heirs to the throne, were raised in the care of their uncle and interim king, Dhritarashtra.

The Pandava brothers grew up as great testaments to goodness and righteousness, while the hundred sons of Dhritarashtra, and in particular Duryodhana, the eldest of the Kaurava brothers, grew up to be greedy, cruel, self-centered, and unscrupulous. Duryodhana was jealous of the Pandavas and tried to destroy them so that he could possess the kingdom, and while Dhritarashtra tried to be impartial, he did nothing to stop or control any of his son's unrighteous ways. Duryodhana sabotaged the rightful ascension of the Pandavas to the throne, banished the Pandavas from the kingdom, and assumed the rulership of the territory. As a result, the kingdom experienced great pain and suffering for many years at the hands of Duryodhana and his unrighteous brothers. Finally the Pandavas had no choice but to take up arms against the Kauravas for the welfare of the kingdom. And so the Gita begins as Arjuna and his charioteer, Krishna, turn to face the Kauravas on the battlefield.

In this profound allegory, Arjuna represents you and me, the spiritual seeker and individualized soul, while Krishna represents the Supreme Soul, the Atman within each of us. The blind king Dhritarashtra represents the blind and undisciplined mind under the spell of ignorance, and his hundred sons the numerous selfish tendencies and forces of negativity that live inside us: greed, anger, fear, self-doubt, lust, jealousy, conceit, possessiveness, and so on. Duryodhana represents the selfish and uncontrolled ego, determined to have its way at all costs and without consideration for others, while the Pandavas represent the highest qualities of goodness, courage, selflessness, wisdom, and love within us.

The kingdom being fought for in the Gita represents the kingdom of the soul within each of us, and the battle, a perennial one, represents the struggle between the power of goodness and the power of selfishness within, and whether the highest or the lowest will be allowed to rule.

The Gita teaches us that if we don't fight against the lower urges within us they will continue to rule over us. Like Duryodhana, they will never just stop. They must *be* stopped, consciously, purposefully, and methodically. We must defeat and destroy them, or they will never relinquish their power over us. The heart and mind must be purified of selfishness and darkness if we are ever to be united with our Highest Self.

It is to this glorious end that the Gita gives us detailed instruction on the spiritual practices available to us in our quest to successfully eliminate the selfishness and negativity within us. The paths to Self-realization that Krishna teaches Arjuna are the four sacred yoga pathways to spiritual union. And the Gita's great promise is that all spiritual aspirants who faithfully follow any or all of these paths will achieve *Moksha*, or liberation from their bondage to the lower, and victory in their struggle to attain to the Highest Good.

PATHWAYS TO UNION:
THE FOUR SCRIPTURAL YOGAS

The four yoga pathways to spiritual union taught in the Gita are built on the profound recognition, made by yoga masters thousands of years ago, that human beings have four faculties through which they can learn to purify the heart, discipline the mind, restrain the senses, and unite with the Self within: the intellect, love, psychic control, and work. Swami Vivekananda describes the four yogas taught in the Gita as such: "Each soul is potentially divine, and the goal of yoga is to manifest this Divinity within by controlling nature, external and internal. We can do this either by work (Karma yoga), or worship (Bhakti yoga), or psychic control (Raja yoga), or knowledge (Jnana yoga) — by one, or more, or all of these, and when we do, we shall be free. Always remember that the bringing forth of the Divinity within us is the whole of religion. Doctrines, or dogmas, or rituals, or books are but secondary details."

Jnana yoga is the path of intellectual discrimination between the real and the unreal. It is the path to union through knowledge, not the mere knowledge of things, but the direct apprehension of the One Infinite Reality *behind* all temporal things. The renunciation of the jnani is the renunciation of all illusions of two-ness. The aim of the jnani is to develop the superconscious ability to see the Divine One everywhere, expressing itself through and as everyone and everything.

Jnana is considered the most difficult of the four yoga pathways, for it calls not only for the rejection of all illusions of duality outside ourselves but also for the rejection of every mental or emotional state within us that hides the truth of Oneness from us. Swami Vivekananda offers us a taste of this:

> As long as you see the many, you are under delusion. "In this world of many, he who sees the One, in this ever-changing world, he who sees Him who never changes as the Soul of his own soul, as his own Self, he is free, he is blessed, he has reached the goal." Therefore, know that you are He; you are one with the God of this universe.
>
> All these small ideas that I am a man or a woman, sick or healthy, strong or weak, or that I hate or love or have little power, are but hallucinations. Stand up then. Know that every thought and word that weakens you in this world is the only evil that exists. Whatever makes you weak and fearful is the only evil that should be shunned. Stand as a rock; you are the Infinite Spirit. Say, "I am Existence Absolute, Bliss Absolute, Knowledge Absolute, I am He," and like a lion breaking its cage, break your chains and be free forever.

Karma yoga is the path of selfless service, the path to union through work offered in the spirit of worship. It is the aim of Karma yoga to sacralize each of our actions through the conscious, constant, and loving offering of our work and the fruits of our work to God. When we work in this way, detached from outcome and in the spirit of service, the bonds of ego-attachment fall away, and our identification with the highest within us grows stronger. Acts of selfless service in devotion to the higher purifies our hearts, destroys our selfishness, and spiritualizes our ego. As Swami Nikhilananda explains:

Behind a man's work there may be different motives. He may work for his own satisfaction, or he may work to please God. In the former case he regards his individualized self as the doer, is elated by success and depressed by failure, and clings to the result. In the latter case he knows that the Lord alone is the Doer, and himself only His instrument; he then works viewing alike success and failure, for the fruit of the action belongs to God alone.

Egocentric action creates bondage for the doer, whereas action performed to please God leads to liberation. Through such action the heart becomes pure, and the man of pure heart acquires the fitness to cultivate Self-knowledge. And through Self-knowledge, he attains liberation. This is called karma yoga, the performance of duty as a yoga.

The renunciation of the Karma yogi is the renunciation of all selfishness and attachment in thought or deed. In this passage from the Bhagavad Gita, Lord Krishna's emphasis on the spiritual power and significance of selfless service is unambiguous:

> Every selfless act, Arjuna,
> is born from Brahman,
> the eternal, infinite Godhead.
> He is present in every act of service.
> All life turns on this law, O Arjuna.
> Whoever violates it,
> indulging his senses for his own pleasure
> and ignoring the needs of others,
> has wasted his life.

Bhakti yoga is the path of love and devotion to a personal God. It is the unceasing adoration of God in any of God's Divine forms:

Heavenly Father, Holy Mother, the Beloved, Christ, Krishna, Shiva, the Lord of Love within, or any embodiment of God that the bhakta can love with all of his or her heart. Through a constant and unbroken flow of adoration directed to God, the bhakta disintegrates all selfishness through the fervor of divine love.

The renunciation of the bhakta is the renunciation of all that is unloving within and all unloving feelings projected outward into the world. The bhakta sees the whole universe as God's and therefore offers unswerving love to all of God's creation. It is through the power of this intense and blissful relationship with God that all the petty desires of the little ego fade away naturally and without struggle, until nothing is left to experience but the Lord of Love Himself. Swami Vivekananda explains:

> Bhakti Yoga is the science of higher love.
> It shows us how to direct love:
> how to manage it, how to use it,
> how to give it a new aim;
> and from it, it shows us how to obtain
> the highest and most glorious results;
> that is, how to make it lead us
> to spiritual blessedness.

> Bhakti yoga does not say, "Give up";
> it only says, "Love the Highest!"
> and everything low
> will naturally fall away from him,
> the object of whose love
> is this Highest.

> What is really required of us in this yoga
> is that our thirst after the beautiful
> should be directed to God.

What is the beauty in the human face,
in the sky, in the stars, and in the moon?
It is only the partial manifestation of the real,
all-embracing Divine Beauty.
"He shining, everything shines."

Raja yoga is the path to union through meditation, concentration, and psychic control. It is for the devotee who is contemplative in nature and who enjoys mining the depths of the soul for the treasure within. The renunciation of the Raja yogi is the renunciation all the mental and emotional states within that hide the glory of the Supreme Soul. Through mastery of Raja yoga comes the complete command of the mind, intellect, and senses, culminating in samadhi, the perfect internal stillness and clarity that reveals the Atman in all its glory. According to the Gita:

Closing their eyes,
steadying their breathing,
and focusing their attention
on the center of spiritual consciousness,
the wise master their senses, mind,
and intellect through meditation.
Self-realization is their only goal.
Freed from selfish desire, fear, and anger,
they live in freedom always.

THE ANTHOLOGY

The Upanishads and the Bhagavad Gita form the foundation wisdom for all subsequent yoga pathways and practices, and that is why yoga teachers throughout history have placed such emphasis on them. Simply stated, they are essential reading for any student of yoga, and no anthology on yoga wisdom would be complete without them. However, each of the four yogas has other scriptures essential to its path as well, and I have included passages from five of them. They include Patanjali's magnificent Yoga Sutras, which is the uncontested bible of Raja yoga; Narada's Bhakti Sutras and the Srimad Bhagavatam, two of the most sacred Bhakti scriptures; the Astavakra Samhita, an important Jnana yoga scripture; and the Dhammapada, the yoga teachings of the blessed Buddha.

And finally, I have included inspired commentary on the yoga scriptures, primarily by Sri Ramakrishna (1836–1886) and Swami Vivekananda (1863–1902), two of India's greatest yoga masters. Ramakrishna, who is considered by millions to be an incarnation of God and the absolute embodiment of all the yoga pathways to Self-realization, is credited with having been the catalyst for the enormous worldwide growth of interest in the wisdom of ancient India since his passing. Swami Vivekananda, whose extraordinary spiritual presence, eloquence, and life of selfless service to humanity continues to make him one of the most beloved yogis in India, will also forever be the father of Western Yoga, the first realized yoga master to bring the great yoga scriptures and teachings to the West at large, first by being the uncontested star of the 1893 World's Parliament of Religions in Chicago, and then, for years afterward, by teaching and spreading the gospel of yoga and Vedanta throughout America and Europe. Two of my favorite testaments to the stature of Ramakrishna and Vivekananda were offered by Sri Aurobindo, one of the most revered yogis of the twentieth century. First regarding Ramakrishna:

> In the life of Ramakrishna we see a colossal spiritual capacity first driving straight to the divine realization, taking the Kingdom of Heaven...and then seizing upon

one yoga method after another and extracting the substance out of it with an incredible rapidity, always to return to the heart of the whole matter, the realization and possession of God by the power of love....His was the great super-conscious life....

And Aurobindo's testament to Vivekananda:

Among all the divisions of mankind it is India...who must send forth from herself the Eternal Religion which is to harmonize all religion, science, and philosophies, and make mankind one soul....It was to initiate this great work...that Bhagawan Ramakrishna came and Vivekananda preached....

The going forth of Vivekananda as the heroic soul destined to take the world between his two hands and change it was the first visible sign that India was awake... He was a power if ever there was one, a very lion among men. We perceive his influence still working gigantically in something grand, intuitive, upheaving.

It is my great hope that the sacred jewels offered in this book will provide the reader with the same kind of joy, illumination, understanding, and spiritual guidance that they have provided to countless lovers of yoga wisdom throughout history, and that these passages will inspire those new to these yoga treasures to pursue the study of the complete scriptures they are drawn from. Please refer to both the recommended books and the acknowledgments sections for suggestions on further study.

I will end this introduction with a wonderful summation of yoga by the blessed Swami Prabhavananda, whose teachings have been particularly valuable to me: "The culmination of all the yogas is the complete unconditional surrender of the lower self, or ego, to God, or the Supreme Self. When the barrier of the ego is removed, by following the path either of knowledge, or of work, or of love, or of meditation, or by following all of them at once, the omnipresent, omniscient, immortal Lord of the universe becomes revealed as the Lord of the heart — the Supreme Self."

Sacred Jewels
of Yoga

CREATION HYMN

തയ.തയ.തയ.തയ

There was not then what is
nor what is not.
There was no sky, and no
heaven beyond the sky.
What power was there? Where?
Who was that power?
Was there an abyss of fathomless waters?

There was neither death nor immortality then.
No signs were there of night or day.
The One was breathing
by its own power, in infinite peace.
Only the One was: there was nothing beyond.

Darkness was hidden in darkness.
The All was fluid and formless.
Therein, in the void,
by the fire of fervor,
arose the One.
And in the One arose love:
Love, the first seed of the soul.
The truth of this the sages found
in their hearts:
seeking in their hearts with wisdom,
the sages found that bond of union
between Being and non-being.

—— RIG VEDA

THE SUPREME TREASURE

Where there is unity,
One without a second,
That is the world of Brahman.
This is the supreme goal of life,
The supreme treasure,
the supreme joy.
Those who do not seek this supreme goal
Live on but a fraction of this joy.

— BRIHADARANYAKA UPANISHAD

For the Sake of the Spirit

The wife loves the husband not for the husband's sake,
but for the sake of the Spirit that is in the husband.

The husband loves the wife not for the wife's sake,
but for the sake of the Spirit that is in the wife.

Children are loved not for the children's sake,
but for the sake of the Spirit that is in the children.

Wealth is loved not for wealth's sake,
but for the sake of the Spirit that is in wealth.

The universe is loved not for the sake of the universe,
but for the sake of the Spirit that is in the universe.

Everything is loved not for its own sake,
but for the sake of the Spirit that lives in it.

This Spirit has to be realized.
Hear about this Spirit and meditate upon Him.
When you hear about the Spirit,
meditate upon the Spirit,
and finally realize the Spirit,
you come to understand everything in life.

— BRIHADARANYAKA UPANISHAD

The Self-Existent

The Lord of Love willed:
"Let me be many!"
And in the depths of His meditation
He created everything that exists.
Meditating, He entered into everything.

He who has no form assumed many forms;
He who is infinite appeared finite;
He who is everywhere assumed a place;
He who is all wisdom caused ignorance;
He who is real caused unreality.

It is He who has become everything.
It is He who gives reality to all.
Before the universe was created,
Brahman existed as unmanifest.
Brahman brought the Lord out of himself;
therefore He is called the Self-existent.

— TAITTIRIYA UPANISHAD

THIS SELF IS BRAHMAN

The Self,
who can be realized by the pure in heart,
who is life, light, truth, space,
who gives rise to all works,
all desires, all tastes,
who is beyond words,
who is joy abiding —
this is the Self dwelling in my heart.

Smaller than a grain of rice,
smaller than a grain of barley,
smaller than a mustard seed,
smaller than a grain of millet,
smaller even than the kernel of
a grain of millet is the Self.
This is the Self dwelling in my heart,
greater than the earth, greater than the sky,
greater than all the worlds.

This Self,
who gives rise to all works, all desires, all tastes,
who pervades the universe,
who is beyond words,
who is joy abiding,
who is ever present in my heart —
This Self is Brahman indeed.
To him I shall attain when my ego dies.

— CHANDOGYA UPANISHAD

WISDOM IN THE SELF

Brahman is the first cause
And the last refuge.
Brahman, the hidden Self in everyone,
does not shine forth.
He is revealed only to those
who keep their mind one-pointed
on the Lord of Love,
and thus develop a superconscious
manner of knowing.

Meditation enables them to go
deeper and deeper into consciousness,
from the world of words,
to the world of thoughts,
then beyond thoughts,
to wisdom in the Self.

— KATHA UPANISHAD

The Eternal One

I know the Self, the sage Shvetashvatara said,
to be immortal and infinite.
I know this Self who is the Self of all,
whom the sages call the Eternal One.

May the Lord of Love, who projects himself
into this universe of myriad forms,
from whom all beings come
and to whom all return,
grant us the grace of wisdom.

He is fire and the sun, and the moon and the stars.
He is the air and the sea, and the Creator, Prajapati.
He is this boy, He is that girl,
He is this man, He is that woman,
and He is this old man, too, tottering on his staff.
His face is everywhere.

He is the blue bird, He is the green bird
with red eyes; He is the thundercloud,
and He is the seasons and the seas.
He has no beginning, He has no end.
He is the source from which the worlds evolve.

From His divine power comes forth all this
magical show of name and form, of you and me,
which casts the spell of pain and pleasure.

Only when we pierce through this
magic veil do we see the
One who appears as many.

— SHVETASHVATARA UPANISHAD

In That Unitive State

⊙⊙.⊙⊙.⊙⊙.⊙⊙

As a man in the arms of his beloved
is not aware of what is without
and what is within,
so a person in union with the Self
is not aware of what is without
and what is within,
for in that unitive state,
all desires find their perfect fulfillment.
There is no other desire
that needs to be fulfilled,
and one goes beyond sorrow.

In that unitive state there is
neither father nor mother,
neither worlds nor gods,
nor even scriptures.
In that state there is neither
thief nor slayer,
neither low caste nor high,
neither monk nor ascetic.
The Self is beyond good and evil,
beyond all the suffering of the human heart.

— BRIHADARANYAKA UPANISHAD

The Lord Is the Supreme Reality

The Lord is enshrined in the hearts of all.
The Lord is the supreme Reality.
Rejoice in him through renunciation.
Covet nothing. All belongs to the Lord.
Thus working may you live a hundred years.
Thus alone will you work in real freedom.

The Self is one. Ever still, the Self is
swifter than thought, swifter than the senses.
Though motionless, he outruns all pursuit.
Without the Self, never could life exist.

The Self seems to move, but is ever still.
He seems far away, but is ever near.
He is within all, and he transcends all.

Those who see all creatures in themselves
and themselves in all creatures know no fear.
Those who see all creatures in themselves
and themselves in all creatures know no grief.
How can the multiplicity of life
delude the one who sees its unity?

—— ISHA UPANISHAD

TWO SELVES

꘠꘠.꘠꘠.꘠꘠.꘠꘠

There are two selves,
the separate ego
and the indivisible Atman.
When one rises above
I and me and mine,
the Atman is revealed
as one's real Self.

When all desires
that surge in the heart
are renounced,
the mortal becomes immortal.
When all the knots
that strangle the heart
are loosened,
the mortal becomes immortal.
This sums up the teaching of the scriptures.

— KATHA UPANISHAD

THE JOY OF THE ATMAN
୭.୭.୭.୭

The joy of the Atman ever abides,
but not what seems pleasant to the senses.
Both these, differing in their purpose,
prompt us to action.
All is well for those who choose
the joy of the Atman,
but they miss the goal of life
who prefer the pleasant.

Perennial joy or passing pleasure?
This is the choice one is to make always.
The wise recognize these two,
but not the ignorant.
The first welcome what leads to abiding joy,
though painful at the time.
The latter run, goaded by their senses,
after what seems immediate pleasure.

— KATHA UPANISHAD

THE HIGHEST MYSTICAL TEACHING

Like oil in sesame seeds, like butter in cream,
like water in springs, like fire in firesticks,
so dwells the Lord of Love, the Self,
in the very depths of consciousness.
Realize Him through truth and meditation.

The Self is hidden in the hearts of all,
as butter lies hidden in cream.
Realize the Self in the depths of meditation —
the Lord of Love, supreme Reality,
who is the goal of all knowledge.

This is the highest mystical teaching;
This is the highest mystical teaching.

May we harness body and mind to see
the Lord of Life, who dwells in everyone.
May we ever with one-pointed mind
strive for blissful union with the Lord.
May we train our senses to serve the Lord
through the practice of meditation.

— SHVETASHVATARA UPANISHAD

THE ONE SELF OF ALL

The Lord of Love
is the one Self of all.
He is detached work,
spiritual wisdom,
and immortality.

Realize the Self
hidden in the heart,
and cut asunder
the knot of ignorance
here and now.

Bright but hidden,
the Self dwells in the heart.
Everything that moves,
breathes, opens, and closes
lives in the Self.

He is the source of love
and may be known through love,
but not through thought.
He is the goal of life.
Attain this goal!

— MUNDAKA UPANISHAD

IN THE HEART MADE PURE

ᕼᕼ᙮ᕼᕼ᙮ᕼᕼ᙮ᕼᕼ

Above the senses is the mind,
above the mind is the intellect,
above that is the ego,
and above the ego
is the unmanifested Cause.

He is formless,
and can never be seen
with these two eyes.
But He reveals Himself
in the heart made pure,
through meditation and sense-restraint.
Realizing Him one is released
from the cycle of birth and death.

When the five senses are stilled,
when the mind is stilled,
when the intellect is stilled,
that is called the highest state by the wise.
They say yoga is this complete stillness,
in which one enters the unitive state,
never to become separate again.

— KATHA UPANISHAD

THE CHARIOT
ᴥ.ᴥ.ᴥ.ᴥ

Know the Self as lord of the chariot,
the body as the chariot itself,
the discriminating intellect as charioteer,
and the mind as reins.
The senses, say the wise, are the horses;
selfish desires are the roads they travel.
When the Self is confused
with the body, mind, and senses,
they point out, He seems
to enjoy pleasure and suffer sorrow.

When one lacks discrimination
and his mind is undisciplined, the senses
run hither and thither like wild horses.
But they obey the rein like trained horses
when one has discrimination
and has made the mind one-pointed.

Those who lack discrimination,
with little control over their thoughts
and far from pure,
reach not the pure state of immortality
but wander from death to death;
but those who have discrimination,
with a still mind and a pure heart,
reach the journey's end,
never again to fall into the jaws of death.

With a discriminating intellect as charioteer
and a trained mind as reins,
they attain the supreme goal of life,
to be united with the Lord of Love.

— KATHA UPANISHAD

AS WE ACT, SO WE BECOME

As a person acts, so he becomes in life.
Those who do good become good;
those who do harm become bad.
Good deeds make one pure;
bad deeds make one impure.

We are said to be what our desire is.
As our desire is, so is our will.
As our will is, so are our acts.
As we act, so we become.

— BRIHADARANYAKA UPANISHAD

The Lord Is the Operator

The Lord is hidden in every heart.
He is the eternal witness,
beyond the gunas,
watching our work from within
as pure consciousness.

The Lord is the operator; we are
but His innumerable instruments.
May we, in our consciousness,
realize the bliss He alone can give us.

Changeless amidst the changing,
consciousness of the conscious,
He grants all our prayers.
May we, in our consciousness,
realize the freedom He alone can give us.

Neither sun nor moon nor star nor fire shines;
everything reflects the light of the Lord.

— SHVETASHVATARA UPANISHAD

The Self Reveals Himself

꘏.꘏.꘏.꘏

Not through discourse,
not through the intellect,
not even through
the study of the scriptures
can the Self be realized.

The Self reveals Himself
to the one who longs for the Self.
Those who long for the Self
with all their heart
are chosen by the Self
as His own.

—— MUNDAKA UPANISHAD

ALL OF LIFE IS ONE

"What is that wisdom, Father?" asked the son.
Uddalaka said to Shvetaketu,

"As by knowing one lump of clay, dear one,
we come to know all things made out of clay:
that they differ only in name and form,
while the stuff of which all are made is clay;

"As by knowing one gold nugget, dear one,
we come to know all things made out of gold:
that they differ only in name and form,
while the stuff of which all are made is gold;

"As by knowing one iron tool, dear one,
we come to know all things made out of iron:
that they differ only in name and form,
while the stuff of which all are made is iron;

"So through that spiritual wisdom, dear one,
we come to know that all of life is one."

— CHANDOGYA UPANISHAD

YOU ARE THAT

❧.❧.❧.❧

Father, please instruct me in this wisdom.
"Yes, dear one, I will," replied his father.

"In the beginning was only Being,
One without a second.
Out of Himself He brought forth the cosmos,
and entered into everything in it.
There is nothing that does not come from Him.
Of everything He is the inmost Self.
He is the truth; He is the Self supreme.
You are that, Shvetaketu; you are that."

— CHANDOGYA UPANISHAD

THE IMMEMORIAL SELF

⌘.⌘.⌘.⌘.⌘

The wise, realizing through meditation
the timeless Self, beyond all perception,
hidden in the cave of the heart,
leave pain and pleasure far behind.

Those who know they are
neither body nor mind
but the immemorial Self,
the divine Principle of existence,
find the source of all joy
and live in joy abiding.

— KATHA UPANISHAD

THE INDIVISIBLE UNITY OF LIFE

As long as there is separateness,
one sees another as separate from oneself,
hears another as separate from oneself,
smells another as separate from oneself,
speaks to another as separate from oneself,
thinks of another as separate from oneself,
knows another as separate from oneself.

But when the Self is realized
as the indivisible unity of life,
who can be seen by whom,
who can be heard by whom,
who can be smelled by whom,
who can be spoken to by whom,
who can be thought of by whom,
who can be known by whom?
Maitreyi, my beloved,
how can the knower ever be known?

— BRIHADARANYAKA UPANISHAD

The Sea of Pure Consciousness

As a lump of salt thrown in water
dissolves and cannot be taken out again,
though wherever we taste the water it is salty,
even so, beloved, the separate self dissolves
in the sea of pure consciousness,
infinite and immortal.

Separateness arises from
identifying the Self with the body,
which is made up of the elements;
when this physical identification dissolves,
there can be no more separate self.
This is what I want to tell you, beloved.

—— BRIHADARANYAKA UPANISHAD

THE PRESENCE OF GOD

All is change in the world of the senses,
but changeless is the supreme Lord of Love.
Meditate on Him, be absorbed in Him,
wake up from this dream of separateness.

Know God and all fetters will fall away.
No longer identifying yourself with the body,
go beyond birth and death.
All your desires will be fulfilled in Him
who is One without a second.

Know Him to be enshrined
in your heart always.
Truly there is nothing more in life to know.
Meditate and realize that this world
is filled with the presence of God.

— SHVETASHVATARA UPANISHAD

THOSE WHO KNOW THE SELF, BECOME THE SELF

What the sages sought
they have found at last.
No more questions
have they to ask of life.
With self-will extinguished,
they are at peace.
Seeing the Lord of Love in all around,
serving the Lord of Love in all around,
they are united with him forever.

They have attained
the summit of wisdom
by the steep path of renunciation.
They have attained to immortality
and are united with the Lord of Love.

When they leave the body,
the vital force returns to the cosmic womb,
but their work becomes a beneficial force in life
to bring others together in the Self.

The flowing river is lost in the sea;
the illumined sage is lost in the Self.
The flowing river has become the sea;
the illumined sage has become the Self.
Those who know the Self,
become the Self.

— MUNDAKA UPANISHAD

Behold the Glory of the Self

❧.❧.❧.❧

Hidden in the heart
of every creature
exists the Self,
subtler than the subtlest,
greater than the greatest.

They go beyond sorrow
who extinguish their self-will
and behold the glory of the Self,
through the grace of the Lord of Love.

— KATHA UPANISHAD

DA-DA-DA!

⁊·⁊·⁊·⁊

The children of Prajapati, the Creator — gods, human beings,
and the godless — lived with their father as students.
When they had completed the allotted period the gods said,
"Venerable One, please teach us."
Prajapati answered with one syllable:
"Da."
"Have you understood?" he asked.
"Yes," they said. "You have told us Damyata,
be self-controlled."
"You have understood," he said.

Then the human beings approached.
"Venerable One, please teach us."
Prajapati answered with one syllable:
"Da."
"Have you understood?" he asked.
"Yes," they said. "You have told us Datta,
give."
"You have understood," he said.

Then the godless approached.
"Venerable One, please teach us."
Prajapati answered with the same syllable:
"Da."
"Have you understood?" he asked.
"Yes," they said. "You have told us Dayadhvam,
be compassionate."
"You have understood," he said.

The heavenly voice of the thunder
repeats this teaching. Da-da-da!
Be self-controlled! Give! Be compassionate!

— BRIHADARANYAKA UPANISHAD

LEARNING AND TEACHING

Practice right conduct,
learning and teaching;

Be truthful always,
learning and teaching;

Master the passions,
learning and teaching;

Control the senses,
learning and teaching;

Strive for peace always,
learning and teaching;

Rouse kundalini,
learning and teaching;

Serve humanity,
learning and teaching.

— TAITTIRIYA UPANISHAD

OM

〰.〰.〰.〰

I will give you the Word that
all the scriptures glorify,
all spiritual disciplines express,
to attain which aspirants lead a life
of sense-restraint and self-naughting.
It is OM.

This symbol of the Godhead is the highest.
Realizing it one finds complete
fulfillment of all one's longings.
It is of the greatest support to all seekers.

Those in whose hearts OM
reverberates unceasingly
are indeed blessed
and deeply loved
as one who is the Self.

— KATHA UPANISHAD

The Effulgent Self

The effulgent Self,
who is beyond thought,
shines in the greatest,
shines in the smallest,
shines in the farthest,
shines in the nearest,
shines in the secret chamber
of the heart.

Beyond the reach
of the senses is He,
but not beyond the reach
of a mind stilled through the
practice of deep meditation.

Beyond the reach of
words and works is He,
but not beyond the reach
of a pure heart
freed from the sway of the senses.

— MUNDAKA UPANISHAD

Two Golden Birds

Like two golden birds
perched on the selfsame tree,
intimate friends,
the ego and the Self dwell in the same body.
The former eats the sweet and sour fruits
of the tree of life,
while the latter looks on in detachment.

As long as we think we are the ego,
we feel attached and fall into sorrow.
But realize that you are the Self,
the Lord of life,
and you will be freed from sorrow.

When you realize that you are the Self,
supreme source of light,
supreme source of love,
you transcend the duality of life
and enter into the unitive state.

— MUNDAKA UPANISHAD

THE LORD OF LOVE

∞.∞.∞.∞

The Lord of Love shines
in the hearts of all.
Seeing Him in all creatures,
the wise forget themselves
in the service of all.

The Lord is their joy,
the Lord is their rest;
such as they are
the lovers of the Lord.

— MUNDAKA UPANISHAD

The World Is the River of God

The world is the wheel of God,
turning round and round
with all living creatures upon its rim.
The world is the river of God,
flowing from him and flowing back to him.

On this ever-revolving wheel of being
the individual self goes round and round,
through life after life,
believing itself to be a separate creature,
until it sees its identity with the Lord of Love
and attains immortality in the indivisible whole.

— SHVETASHVATARA UPANISHAD

REALITY LIES IN THE ETERNAL
⁓.⁓.⁓.⁓

The impermanent has no reality;
reality lies in the eternal.
Those who have seen the
boundary between these two have
attained the end of all knowledge.

Realize that which pervades
the universe, and is indestructible;
no power can affect this
unchanging, imperishable reality.
The body is mortal,
but He who dwells in the body is
immortal and immeasurable.

— BHAGAVAD GITA

THE YOGA OF WORKS

Every selfless act, Arjuna,
is born from Brahman,
the eternal, infinite Godhead.
He is present in every act of service.
All life turns on this law, O Arjuna.
Whoever violates it,
indulging his senses for his own pleasure
and ignoring the needs of others,
has wasted his life.

But those who realize the Self
are always satisfied.
Having found the source of
joy and fulfillment,
they no longer seek happiness
from the external world.
They have nothing to gain
or lose by any action;
neither people nor things
can affect their security.

Strive constantly to serve
the welfare of the world;
by devotion to selfless work one
attains the supreme goal of life.
Do your work with the
welfare of others always in mind.

—— BHAGAVAD GITA

ENEMY THAT IS SELFISH DESIRE

ᖇᖇ·ᖇᖇ·ᖇᖇ·ᖇᖇ

ARJUNA
What is the force that binds us to selfish deeds, O Krishna?
What power moves us, even against our will, as if forcing us?

KRISHNA
It is selfish desire and anger,
arising from the guna of rajas;
These are the appetites and evils which
threaten a person in this life.

Just as a fire is covered by smoke
and a mirror is obscured by dust,
just as the embryo rests deep within the womb,
knowledge is hidden by selfish desire — hidden, Arjuna,
by this unquenchable fire for self-satisfaction,
the inveterate enemy of the wise.

Selfish desire is found in the
senses, mind, and intellect, misleading them and
burying the understanding in delusion.
Fight with all your strength, Arjuna!
Controlling your senses, conquer your enemy,
the destroyer of knowledge and realization.

The senses are higher than the body,
the mind higher than the senses;
above the mind is the intellect,
and above the intellect is the Atman.
Thus, knowing that which is supreme,
let the Atman rule the ego.
Use your mighty arms to slay the
fierce enemy that is selfish desire.

— BHAGAVAD GITA

ALL PATHS LEAD TO ME
◦◦.◦◦.◦◦.◦◦

My true being is unborn and changeless.
I am the Lord who dwells in every creature.
Through the power of my own maya,
I manifest myself in a finite form.

Whenever dharma declines
and the purpose of life is forgotten,
I manifest myself on earth.
I am born in every age to protect the good,
to destroy evil, and to re-establish dharma.

He who knows me as his own divine Self
breaks through the belief that he is the body
and is not reborn as a separate creature.
Such a one, Arjuna, is united with me.
Delivered from selfish attachment, fear, and anger,
filled with me, surrendering themselves to me,
purified in the fire of my being,
many have reached the state of unity in me.

As men approach me, so I receive them.
All paths, Arjuna, lead to me.

— BHAGAVAD GITA

TRUE SUSTENANCE IS IN SERVICE

True sustenance is in service,
and through it a man or woman
reaches the eternal Brahman.
But those who do not seek to serve
are without a home in this world.
Arjuna, how can they be at home
in any world to come?

These offerings are born of work,
and each guides mankind
along a path to Brahman.
Understanding this,
you will attain liberation.

The offering of wisdom is better
than any material offering, Arjuna;
for the goal of all work is spiritual wisdom.

Approach someone who has
realized the purpose of life
and question him with
reverence and devotion;
he will instruct you in this wisdom.
Once you attain it, you
will never again be deluded.
You will see all creatures in the Self,
and all in me.

— BHAGAVAD GITA

Take Up the Path of Yoga!

Nothing in this world purifies
like spiritual wisdom.
It is the perfection achieved in time
through the path of yoga,
the path which leads to the Self within.

Those who take wisdom
as their highest goal,
whose faith is deep and
whose senses are trained,
attain wisdom quickly and enter
into perfect peace.
But the ignorant, indecisive and
lacking in faith, waste their lives.
They can never be happy
in this world or any other.

Those established in the Self
have renounced selfish
attachments to their actions,
and cut through doubts
with spiritual wisdom.
They act in freedom.

Arjuna, cut through this doubt
in your own heart with the
sword of spiritual wisdom.
Arise: take up the path of yoga!

— BHAGAVAD GITA

Free from the Bondage of Self-Will

Those who have attained perfect renunciation
are free from any sense of duality;
they are unaffected by likes and dislikes, Arjuna,
and are free from the bondage of self-will.

The immature think that knowledge
and action are different,
but the wise see them as the same.
The person who is established in one path
will attain the rewards of both.

The goal of knowledge
and the goal of service are the same;
those who fail to see this are blind.

Perfect renunciation is difficult to attain
without performing action.
But the wise,
following the path of selfless service,
quickly reach Brahman.

Those who follow the path of service,
who have completely purified themselves
and conquered their senses and self-will,
see the Self in all creatures and are untouched
by any action they perform.

— BHAGAVAD GITA

SHINES LIKE THE SUN

Judgment is clouded when
wisdom is obscured by ignorance.
But ignorance is destroyed
by knowledge of the Self within.
The light of this knowledge
shines like the sun,
revealing the supreme Brahman.

Those who cast off sin
through this knowledge,
absorbed in the Lord and
established in Him as their
one goal and refuge,
are not reborn as separate creatures.

Those who possess this wisdom
have equal regard for all.
They see the same Self
in a spiritual aspirant and an outcaste,
in an elephant, a cow, and a dog.
Such people have mastered life.
With even mind they rest in Brahman,
who is perfect and is everywhere the same.

— BHAGAVAD GITA

TRUE RENUNCIATION

It is not those who lack energy or refrain from action,
but those who work without expectation of reward
who attain the goal of meditation.
Theirs is true renunciation.

Therefore, Arjuna, you should understand
that renunciation and the performance
of selfless service are the same.
Those who cannot renounce attachment
to the results of their work are far from the path.

For aspirants who want to
climb the mountain of spiritual awareness,
the path is selfless work;
for those who have ascended to yoga,
the path is stillness and peace.

When a person has freed himself
from attachment to the results of work,
and from desires for the enjoyment of sense objects,
he ascends to the unitive state.

— BHAGAVAD GITA

RESHAPE YOURSELF

ᘓᕲ.ᘓᕲ.ᘓᕲ.ᘓᕲ

Reshape yourself
through the power of your will;
never let yourself be degraded by self-will.

The will is the only friend of the Self,
and the will is the only enemy of the Self.
To those who have conquered themselves,
the will is a friend.
But the will is the enemy of those who
have not found the Self within them.

The supreme Reality stands revealed
in the consciousness of those
who have conquered themselves.
They live in peace, alike in cold and heat,
pleasure and pain, praise and blame.

— BHAGAVAD GITA

MEDITATION

৹৹.৹৹.৹৹.৹৹

Those who aspire to the state of yoga
should seek the Self in inner solitude
through meditation.

With body and mind controlled,
they should constantly practice one-pointedness,
free from expectations and
attachment to material possessions.

Select a clean spot, neither too high nor too low,
and seat yourself firmly on a cloth,
a deerskin, and kusha grass.
Then, once seated, strive to still your thoughts.

Make your mind one-pointed in meditation,
and your heart will be purified.
Hold your body, head, and neck
firmly in a straight line,
and keep your eyes from wandering.

With all fears dissolved in the peace of the Self
and all desires dedicated to Brahman,
controlling the mind and fixing it on me,
sit in meditation with me as your only goal.

With senses and mind constantly
controlled through meditation,
united with the Self within,
an aspirant attains nirvana,
the state of abiding joy and peace in me.

— BHAGAVAD GITA

IN THE STILL MIND

@ꞔ.@ꞔ.@ꞔ.@ꞔ

When meditation is mastered,
the mind is unwavering like the
flame of a lamp in a windless place.

In the still mind,
in the depths of meditation,
the Self reveals itself.
Beholding the Self
by means of the Self,
an aspirant knows the
joy and peace of complete fulfillment.

Having attained that
abiding joy beyond the senses,
revealed in the stilled mind,
he never swerves from the eternal truth.

— BHAGAVAD GITA

THE PATH OF YOGA

The practice of meditation
frees one from all affliction.
This is the path of yoga.
Follow it with determination
and sustained enthusiasm.

Renouncing wholeheartedly all
selfish desires and expectations,
use your will to control the senses.
Little by little, through
patience and repeated effort,
the mind will become stilled in the Self.

Wherever the mind wanders,
restless and diffuse in its search
for satisfaction without,
lead it within;
train it to rest in the Self.

Abiding joy comes
to those who still the mind.
Freeing themselves
from the taint of self-will,
with their consciousness unified,
they become one with Brahman.

— BHAGAVAD GITA

I Am Ever Present

෨෨.෨෨.෨෨.෨෨

I am ever present to those
who have realized me in every creature.
Seeing all life
as my manifestation,
they are never
separated from me.

They worship me
in the hearts of all,
and all their actions
proceed from me.
Wherever they may live,
they abide in me.

When a person responds
to the joys and sorrows of others
as if they were his own,
he has attained the highest
state of spiritual union.

— BHAGAVAD GITA

My Necklace of Jewels

There is nothing that exists
separate from me, Arjuna.
The entire universe is suspended from me
as my necklace of jewels.

Arjuna, I am the taste of pure water
and the radiance of the sun and moon.
I am the sacred word, the sound heard in air,
and the courage of human beings.

I am the sweet fragrance in the earth
and the radiance of fire;
I am the life in every creature
and the striving of the spiritual aspirant.

My eternal seed, Arjuna,
is to be found in every creature.
I am the power of discrimination
in those who are intelligent,
and the glory of the noble.
In those who are strong, I am strength,
free from passion and selfish attachment.

I am desire itself, if that desire
is in harmony with the purpose of life.

—— BHAGAVAD GITA

That One Is Me

ᕙ.ᕙ.ᕙ.ᕙ

Truly great souls
seek my divine nature.
They worship me
with a one-pointed mind,
having realized that
I am the eternal source of all.

Constantly striving,
they make firm their resolve,
and they worship me without wavering.
Full of devotion,
they sing of my divine glory.

Others follow the path of jnana,
spiritual wisdom.
They see that where there is One,
that One is me;
where there are many,
all are me;
they see my face everywhere.

— BHAGAVAD GITA

I Am

I am the ritual and the sacrifice;
I am true medicine and the mantra.
I am the offering and
the fire which consumes it,
and he to whom it is offered.

I am the father and
mother of this universe,
and its grandfather too;
I am its entire support.
I am the sum of all knowledge,
the purifier, the syllable OM.

I am the sacred scriptures,
the Rig, Yajur, and Sama Vedas.
I am the goal of life,
the Lord and support of all,
the inner witness, the abode of all.

I am the only refuge,
the one true friend;
I am the beginning, the staying,
and the end of creation.

I am the womb and the eternal seed.
I am heat; I give and withhold the rain.

I am immortality and I am death;
I am what is and what is not.

— BHAGAVAD GITA

THOSE WHO WORSHIP ME

Whatever I am offered in devotion
with a pure heart —
a leaf, a flower, fruit, or water —
I partake of that love offering.

Whatever you do,
make it an offering to me —
the food you eat, the sacrifices you make,
the help you give, even your suffering.

In this way you will be freed
from the bondage of karma,
and from its results,
both pleasant and painful.
Then, firm in renunciation and yoga,
with your heart free,
you will come to me.

I look upon all creatures equally;
none are less dear to me
and none more dear.
But those who worship me with love
live in me,
and I come to life in them.

— BHAGAVAD GITA

Worship Me Always

All those who
take refuge in me,
whatever their birth,
race, sex, or caste,
will attain the supreme goal;
this realization can be attained
even by those whom society scorns.
Kings and sages too seek
this goal with devotion.

Therefore, having been born in this
transient and forlorn world,
give all your love to me.
Fill your mind with me;
love me; serve me;
worship me always.
Seeking me in your heart,
you will at last be united with me.

— BHAGAVAD GITA

Surrender Yourself to Me

꿍.꿍.꿍.꿍

Still your mind in me,
still your intellect in me,
and without doubt you will be
united with me forever.

If you cannot still your mind in me,
learn to do so through
the regular practice of meditation.

If you lack the will for such self-discipline,
engage yourself in my work,
for selfless service can lead you
at last to complete fulfillment.

If you are unable to do even this,
surrender yourself to me,
disciplining yourself
and renouncing the results
of all your actions.

— BHAGAVAD GITA

My Devotee

꩜.꩜.꩜.꩜

That one I love,
who is incapable of ill will,
is friendly and compassionate.
Living beyond the reach of I and mine,
of pleasure and pain,
patient, contented, self-controlled,
with all his heart and all his mind
given to me —
With such a one I am in love.

Not agitating the world
or by it agitated,
he stands above the sway of
elation, competition, and fear;
he is my beloved.

He is detached, pure, efficient,
impartial, never anxious,
selfless in all his undertakings;
he is my devotee, very dear to me.

— BHAGAVAD GITA

Show Good Will to All

꩜.꩜.꩜.꩜

Be fearless and pure;
never waver in your determination or
your dedication to the spiritual life.
Give freely. Be self-controlled,
sincere, truthful, loving,
and full of the desire to serve.

Realize the truth of the scriptures;
learn to be detached and to
take joy in renunciation.
Do not get angry or
harm any living creature,
but be compassionate and gentle;
show good will to all.

Cultivate vigor, patience, will, purity;
avoid malice and pride.
Then, Arjuna, you will achieve
your divine destiny.

— BHAGAVAD GITA

PERFECTION

By devotion to
one's own particular duty,
everyone can attain perfection.
Let me tell you how.

By performing his own work,
one worships the Creator
who dwells in every creature.
Such worship brings that person
to fulfillment.

It is better to perform
one's own duties imperfectly
than to master the duties of another.
By fulfilling the obligations
he is born with,
a person never comes to grief.

— BHAGAVAD GITA

BY LOVING ME

Listen and I shall explain now, Arjuna,
how one who has attained perfection
also attains Brahman,
the supreme consummation of wisdom.

Unerring in his discrimination,
sovereign of his senses and passions,
free from the clamor of likes and dislikes,
he leads a simple, self-reliant life,
based on meditation, controlling
his speech, body, and mind.

Free from self-will,
aggressiveness, arrogance, anger,
and the lust to possess people or things,
he is at peace with himself and others,
and enters into the unitive state.

United with Brahman, ever joyful,
beyond the reach of desire and sorrow,
he has equal regard for every living creature
and attains supreme devotion to me.

By loving me he comes to know me truly;
then he knows my glory and
enters into my boundless being.

All his acts are performed in my service,
and through my grace he wins eternal life.

— BHAGAVAD GITA

Make Every Act an Offering to Me

I give you these precious
words of wisdom;
reflect on them,
and then do as you choose.
These are the last words
I shall speak to you for
your spiritual fulfillment.
You are very dear to me.

Be aware of me always, adore me,
make every act an offering to me,
and you shall come to me;
this I promise;
for you are dear to me.

Abandon all supports,
and look to me for protection.
I shall purify you.

— BHAGAVAD GITA

HOW CAN LIBERATION BE ATTAINED?

How can knowledge be acquired?
How can liberation be attained?
How is renunciation possible?
Tell me this, O Lord.

If you aspire after liberation, my child,
free yourself from the objects of the senses
and seek forgiveness, sincerity, kindness,
contentment, and truth as nectar.

You are neither earth, nor water,
nor fire, nor air, nor space.
In order to attain liberation,
know the Self as the witness of all these,
and as Consciousness Itself.

If you detach yourself from the body,
and rest in Consciousness,
you will at once be happy, peaceful,
and free from bondage.

— ASTAVAKRA SAMHITA

You Are the One

Virtue and vice, pleasure and pain
are of the mind, and not of you,
O all-pervading one.
You are neither doer nor enjoyer.
Verily you are ever free.

You are the one seer of all.
Verily this alone is your bondage;
that you see yourself not as the seer,
but as something other.

You who have been bitten by the
great black serpent of the egoism,
"I am the doer."
Drink the nectar of the faith,
"I am not the doer,"
and be happy.

Burn down the forest of ignorance
with the fire of the conviction,
"I am the One, I am Pure Consciousness,"
and be free from grief.

—— ASTAVAKRA SAMHITA

As One Thinks, So One Becomes

∞·∞·∞·∞

You are Consciousness,
Bliss Supreme,
in and upon which this universe
appears superimposed,
like a snake on a rope.

He who considers himself free
is free indeed,
and he who considers himself bound,
remains bound.
"As one thinks, so one becomes"
is a popular saying in this world,
and it is quite true.

— ASTAVAKRA SAMHITA

THE SELF IS WITNESS

The Self is witness,
all-pervading, perfect,
One, free, actionless,
unattached, desireless, and quiet.

Through illusion it appears
as if the Self is of the world,
subject to the ever-repeating
cycle of birth and death.

Having given up external
and internal self-modifications,
and the illusion
"I am the reflected individual self,"
meditate on the Atman as immutable,
Consciousness, and non-dual.

— ASTAVAKRA SAMHITA

Desire Consciousness Alone

My child, you have long been caught
in the noose of body-consciousness.
Sever it with the sword of the knowledge,
"I am Consciousness,"
and be happy.

You are unattached, actionless,
self-effulgent, and without blemish.
You pervade this universe,
and this universe exists in you.
You are Pure Consciousness by nature.
Do not be small-minded.

You are unconditioned, immutable,
formless, and of unfathomable intelligence.
Desire Consciousness alone.

— ASTAVAKRA SAMHITA

Brahman Exists in All Things

Know that which has form to be unreal
and the formless to be permanent.
Through this spiritual instruction
you will escape the possibility of rebirth.

Just as a mirror exists
within and without
the image reflected in it,
so the Supreme Self exists
inside and outside this body.

Just as the same all-pervading space
is inside and outside a jar,
so the eternal, all-pervasive
Brahman exists in all things.

—— ASTAVAKRA SAMHITA

NOTHING BUT THE SELF

ᘔᘔ.ᘔᘔ.ᘔᘔ.ᘔᘔ

As waves, foam, and bubbles
are not different from water,
so the universe emanating from the Self
is not different from It.

As cloth, when analyzed,
is found to be nothing but thread,
so this universe, when analyzed,
is nothing but the Self.

—— ASTAVAKRA SAMHITA

LIGHT IS MY VERY NATURE

Light is my very nature.
I am no other than light.
When the universe manifests itself,
verily then it is I that shines.

Oh, the universe appears in me,
conceived through ignorance,
just as silver appears
in the mother of pearl,
a snake in the rope,
and the mirage in the sunbeam.

Just as a jug dissolves into clay,
a wave into water,
and a bracelet into gold,
so the universe,
which has emanated from me,
will dissolve into me.

— ASTAVAKRA SAMHITA

I Am the Stainless Self

Knowledge, knower, and the knowable —
these three do not exist in reality.
I am that stainless Self in which
this triad appears through ignorance.

The root of misery is duality.
There is no other remedy for it,
except the realization that
all objects of experience are unreal,
and that I am pure,
One, Consciousness, and Bliss.

I am Pure Consciousness.
Through ignorance,
I have imposed limitations upon myself.
Constantly reflecting in this way,
I am abiding in the Absolute.

— ASTAVAKRA SAMHITA

THE SHORELESS OCEAN

In me, the limitless ocean,
on the rising of the wind of the mind,
diverse waves of worlds are produced.

With the calming of the wind of the mind,
in the infinite ocean of myself,
the seeming self vanishes.

How wonderful!
In me, the shoreless ocean,
the waves of individual selves,
according to their nature,
rise, strike each other,
play for a time, and then disappear.

— ASTAVAKRA SAMHITA

THIS IS KNOWLEDGE
๛.๛.๛.๛

Boundless as space am I,
and the phenomenal world is like a jar.
This is Knowledge.
So it has neither to be renounced,
nor accepted, nor destroyed.

I am like the ocean and
the universe is like the wave.
This is Knowledge.
So it has neither to be renounced,
nor accepted, nor destroyed.

I am indeed in all beings,
and all beings are in me.
This is Knowledge.
So it has neither to be renounced,
nor accepted, nor destroyed.

— ASTAVAKRA SAMHITA

BLISS ITSELF

Give up such distinctions as
"I am He" and "I am not this."
Consider all as the Self
and be desireless and happy.

In reality you are One.
There is no individual self
or Supreme Self
other than you.

One who knows for certain that
this universe is but an illusion, a nothing,
becomes desireless and Pure Intelligence,
and finds peace.

In the ocean of the world
One only was, is, and will be.
You have neither bondage nor liberation.
Live contented and happily.

O Pure Intelligence,
do not disturb your mind
with affirmations and negations.
Be calm and abide happily in your own self,
which is Bliss itself.

— ASTAVAKRA SAMHITA

Oh, Knower of Truth

The knower of Truth is never miserable in this world,
for the whole universe is filled by himself alone.

Rare indeed is the great-souled one,
who is not desirous of either
enjoyment or liberation.

Rare is the broad-minded person
who has neither attraction for, nor aversion to duty,
world prosperity, desire, or liberation.

The man of knowledge does not feel any desire
for the dissolution of the universe,
or aversion to its existence.
The blessed one, therefore,
lives happily on whatever sustenance comes
as a matter of course.

Being fulfilled by the knowledge of the Self,
and with his mind absorbed and contented,
the wise one lives happily,
seeing, hearing, touching, smelling, and eating.

— ASTAVAKRA SAMHITA

The Liberated One

~·~·~·~

The liberated one
is always found abiding in the Self
and is pure in heart;
he lives freed from all desires,
under all conditions.

The liberated one
neither slanders nor praises,
neither rejoices nor is angry.
He is free from attachment to all objects.

The liberated one
neither abhors the objects of the senses
nor craves them.
Ever with a detached mind
he experiences them as they come.

Devoid of the feeling of "I" and "mine,"
knowing for certain that nothing is,
with all his inner desires set at rest,
the person of knowledge does not act,
though he may be acting.

— ASTAVAKRA SAMHITA

He Who Has Transcended All

This universe is but
a state of consciousness.
In reality it is nothing.
The existent and the non-existent
do not lose their inherent nature.

The Self which is absolute, effortless,
immutable, and spotless
is neither far away nor limited.
It is verily ever attained.

Such thoughts as
"this indeed am I" and "this I am not"
are annihilated for the yogi
who has become silent by
knowing for certain all as the Self.

He who has seen
the Supreme Brahman
meditates,
"I am Brahman."
But what does he who
has transcended all thought think,
when he sees no second?

— ASTAVAKRA SAMHITA

As Brahman Itself

There is no joy or sorrow
for one who has
transcended worldly existence.
Ever with a serene mind,
he lives like one without a body.

The wise man who delights in the Self,
and whose mind is calm and pure,
has no desire to renounce anything whatsoever,
nor does he feel any loss anywhere.

As the wise one has no distraction,
he is neither an aspirant for liberation
nor is he in bondage.
Having known the universe to be a figment
even though he sees it,
he exists as Brahman itself.

— ASTAVAKRA SAMHITA

THE WISE ONE

Some think that existence is,
and others that nothing is.
Rare is the one who thinks neither,
and is thus calm.

The wise one does freely
whatever comes to be done;
his actions are like those of a child.

The conduct of the wise one,
which is unrestricted by motive, shines,
being free from pretense.

— ASTAVAKRA SAMHITA

The Knower of the Self

With perfect equanimity,
even in practical life,
the wise one sits happily,
sleeps happily, moves happily,
speaks happily, and eats happily.

With the deluded,
even inaction becomes action;
and with the wise, even action results
in the fruit of inaction.

The wise one who has no motive in all his actions,
who moves like a child and is pure,
has no attachment even to the work
that is being done by him.

Blessed indeed is that knower of the Self
who has transcended the mind,
and who, even though seeing, hearing,
touching, smelling, or eating,
is the same under all conditions.

— ASTAVAKRA SAMHITA

The Yogi of Indescribable Nature

❦·❦·❦·❦

The wise one lives without the feeling of
"I-ness" and "mine-ness" and attachment.

To the wise one
who perceives the Self
as imperishable and free from grief,
where is knowledge and where is the universe?
Where is the feeling "I am the body,"
or "the body is mine"?

For the wise one
who is ever immutable and fearless,
where is there darkness, where light?
Where, moreover, is there any loss?

Where is patience,
where is discrimination,
and where, even, is fearlessness
for the yogi of indescribable nature.

— ASTAVAKRA SAMHITA

YOGIC CONSCIOUSNESS

There is no heaven, and there is no hell;
there is not even liberation in life.
In short, nothing exists but the Self.

The wise one neither longs for gain
nor grieves at non-attainment.
His cool mind is verily filled
with the nectar of Supreme Bliss.

Glorious is the wise one
who is devoid of the feeling of "mine,"
to whom the earth, a stone, and gold are all the same,
the knots of whose heart have been rent asunder.

Where is wantonness, where is restraint,
and where is determination of Truth
for the yogi whose life's object has been fulfilled
and who is the embodiment of guileless sincerity?

Praised, the wise one does not feel pleased;
blamed, he does not feel annoyed.
He neither rejoices in life, nor fears death.

The tranquil-minded one seeks
neither the crowded place nor the wilderness.
He remains the same,
under any conditions, and in any place.

— ASTAVAKRA SAMHITA

ONE WHO SHINES AS THE INFINITE

Glorious are those who are free from all desires,
who are the perfect embodiments of bliss
which is their true nature,
and who are spontaneously absorbed
in the unconditioned Self.

In short, the great-souled ones,
who have realized the Truth
are free from the desire for
enjoyment and liberation,
and are devoid of all attachment
at all times and in all places.

The pure ones know for certain that
this universe is the product of illusion,
and that nothing exists.
The imperceptible Self is revealed to them,
and they naturally enjoy peace.

Rules of conduct, dispassion, renunciation,
and restraint of the senses —
what are all these to those
who are of the nature
of Pure Effulgence?

Where is bondage or liberation, joy or sorrow
for one who shines as the Infinite?

— ASTAVAKRA SAMHITA

GO ABOUT HAPPILY

Non-attachment to sense-objects is liberation;
love for sense-objects is bondage.
Such verily is Knowledge.
Now do as you please.

You are not the body, nor is the body yours;
you are not the doer, nor the enjoyer.
You are Consciousness itself,
the eternal Witness, ever free.
Go about happily.

Attachment and abhorrence
are attributes of the mind.
The mind is never yours.
You are Intelligence itself,
free from conflict, and changeless.
Go about happily.

Realizing the Self in all
and all in the Self,
free from egoism
and the sense of "mine,"
go about happily.

— ASTAVAKRA SAMHITA

Knowledge of the Atman

∽.∽.∽.∽

This is the beginning of instruction in yoga.
Yoga is the control of thought-waves in the mind.
Then man abides in his real nature.

At other times, when he is not
in the state of yoga,
man remains identified with the
thought-waves in the mind.

Practice is the repeated effort
to follow the disciplines
which give permanent control
of the thought waves of the mind.

Practice becomes firmly grounded
when it has been cultivated for a long time,
uninterruptedly, with earnest devotion.

— PATANJALI'S YOGA SUTRAS

Non-attachment

༄༅.༄༅.༄༅.༄༅

Non-attachment is self-mastery;
it is freedom from desire
for what is seen or heard.

When, through knowledge
of the Atman,
one ceases to desire
any manifestation of Nature,
then that is the highest kind
of non-attachment.

— PATANJALI'S YOGA SUTRAS

THE WORD THAT EXPRESSES HIM IS OM

The concentration of the
true spiritual aspirant is attained
through faith, energy, recollectedness,
absorption, and illumination.

Success in yoga comes quickly
to those who are intensely energetic.

Concentration may also be attained
through devotion to God, Ishwara.

Ishwara is a special kind of being,
untouched by ignorance
and the products of ignorance,
not subject to karmas or samskaras
or the results of action.
In Him, knowledge is infinite;
in others it is only a germ.

He was the teacher
even of the earliest teachers,
since He is not limited by time.
The word that expresses Him is OM.
This word must be repeated
with meditation upon its meaning.

Hence comes knowledge of the Atman
and destruction of the obstacles to that knowledge.

— PATANJALI'S YOGA SUTRAS

THE MANY PATHS TO FREEDOM

Sickness, mental laziness,
doubt, lack of enthusiasm, sloth,
craving for sense pleasure, false perception,
despair caused by failure to concentrate,
and unsteadiness in concentration:
these distractions are the
obstacles to knowledge.

They can be removed
by the practice of concentration
upon a single truth.

Undisturbed calmness of mind
is attained by cultivating
friendliness toward the happy,
compassion for the unhappy,
delight in the virtuous, and
indifference toward the wicked.

— PATANJALI'S YOGA SUTRAS

CONCENTRATION

∾.∾.∾.∾

The mind may be calmed by
expulsion and retention of the breath.

Concentration may also be attained by
fixing the mind upon the Inner Light,
which is beyond sorrow.

Or by meditating on the heart
of an illumined soul,
that is free from passion.

Or by fixing the mind upon
any divine form or symbol
that appeals to one as good.

— PATANJALI'S YOGA SUTRAS

The Obstacles

Austerity, study, and the dedication of
the fruits of one's work to God:
these are the preliminary steps
toward yoga.

Thus we may cultivate
the power of concentration
and remove the obstacles
to enlightenment
which cause all our sufferings.

These obstacles —
the causes of man's sufferings —
are ignorance, egoism, attachment, aversion,
and the desire to cling to life.

Ignorance creates
all the other obstacles.

— PATANJALI'S YOGA SUTRAS

Ignorance and Egoism

To regard the non-eternal as eternal,
the impure as pure,
the painful as pleasant,
and the non-Atman as the Atman —
this is ignorance.

To identify consciousness with
that which merely reflects consciousness —
this is egoism.

Attachment is that which dwells upon pleasure.
Aversion is that which dwells upon pain.

The desire to cling to life is inherent
both in the ignorant and in the learned.
This is because the mind retains
impressions of the death experience
from many previous incarnations.

When these obstacles
have been reduced to a vestigial form,
they can be destroyed,
by resolving the mind back
into its primal cause.

In their fully developed form,
they can be overcome through meditation.

— PATANJALI'S YOGA SUTRAS

False Identification

A man's latent tendencies have been created
by his past thoughts and actions.
These tendencies will bear fruits,
both in this life and in lives to come.

So long as the cause exists, it will bear fruits —
such as rebirth, a long or a short life,
and the experiences of pleasure and of pain.

Experiences of pleasure and pain
are the fruits of merit and demerit, respectively.

But the man of spiritual discrimination
regards all these experiences as painful.
For even the enjoyment of the
present pleasure is painful,
since we already fear its loss.
Past pleasure is painful
because renewed cravings arise
from the impressions
it has left upon the mind.

And how can any happiness be lasting
if it depends only upon our moods?
For these moods are constantly changing,
as one or another of the ever-warring gunas
seizes control of the mind.

— PATANJALI'S YOGA SUTRAS

KNOWLEDGE OF THE ATMAN

The Atman — the experiencer —
is pure consciousness.
It appears to take on the
changing colors of the mind.
In reality, it is unchangeable.

The object of experience exists only to
serve the purpose of the Atman.

Though the object of experience becomes unreal
to those who have reached the state of liberation,
it remains real to all other beings.

The Atman — the experiencer —
is identified with
Prakriti — the objects of experience —
in order that the true nature of both
Prakriti and Atman may be known.

This identification is caused by ignorance.
When ignorance has been destroyed,
this identification ceases.
Then bondage is at an end
and the experiencer is independent and free.

Ignorance is destroyed by awakening
to knowledge of the Atman,
until no trace of illusions remains.

— PATANJALI'S YOGA SUTRAS

THE EIGHT LIMBS OF YOGA

As soon as all impurities have been removed
by the practice of the spiritual disciplines —
the "limbs" of yoga —
an aspirant's spiritual vision opens to the
light-giving knowledge of the Atman.

The eight limbs of yoga are:
The various forms of abstention from evil-doing (yama),
the various observances (niyama),
posture (asana),
control of the prana (pranayama),
withdrawal of the mind from sense objects (pratyahara),
concentration (dharana),
meditation (dhyana), and
absorption in the Atman (samadhi).

— PATANJALI'S YOGA SUTRAS

YAMA AND NIYAMA

Yama is abstention from harming others,
from falsehood, from theft,
from incontinence, and from greed.

The niyamas are purity,
contentment, austerity,
study, and devotion to God.

To be free from thoughts that
distract one from yoga,
thoughts of an opposite kind
must be cultivated.

The obstacles to yoga —
such as acts of violence and untruth —
may be directly created,
or indirectly caused or approved;
they may be motivated by
greed, anger, or self-interest;
they may be small or moderate or great —
but they never cease to result in
pain and ignorance.
One should overcome distracting thoughts
by remembering this.

— PATANJALI'S YOGA SUTRAS

STEADFASTNESS

When a man becomes steadfast
in his abstention from harming others,
then all living creatures will
cease to feel enmity in his presence.

When a man becomes steadfast
in his abstention from falsehood,
he gets the power of obtaining for himself and others
the fruits of good deeds,
without having to perform the deeds themselves.

When a man becomes steadfast
in his abstention from theft,
all wealth comes to him.

When a man becomes steadfast
in his abstention from incontinence,
he acquires spiritual energy.

Moreover, one achieves
purification of the heart,
cheerfulness of mind,
the power of concentration,
control of the passions,
and fitness for vision of the Atman.

As the result of contentment,
one gains supreme happiness.

As the result of devotion to God,
one achieves samadhi.

— PATANJALI'S YOGA SUTRAS

Asana, Pranayama, and Pratyahara
෮෮.෮෮.෮෮.෮෮

Posture (asana) is to be seated
in a position which is firm but relaxed.

Posture becomes firm and relaxed through
control of the natural tendencies of the body,
and through meditation on the infinite.
Thereafter, one is no longer troubled
by the dualities of sense experience.

After mastering posture, one must practice
control of prana (pranayama).

As the result of this,
the covering of the Inner Light is removed.

The mind then gains the power of concentration (dharana).

When the mind is withdrawn from sense-objects,
the sense-organs also withdraw themselves
from their respective objects.
This is known as pratyahara.

Thence arises complete mastery over the senses.

— PATANJALI'S YOGA SUTRAS

Concentration, Meditation, and Absorption

Concentration (dharana)
is holding the mind within a center
of spiritual consciousness in the body,
or fixing it on some divine form,
either within the body or outside it.

Meditation (dhyana)
is an unbroken flow of thought
toward the object of concentration.

When, in meditation,
the true nature of the object shines forth,
not distorted by the mind of the perceiver,
that is absorption (samadhi).

When these three —
concentration, meditation, and absorption —
are brought to bear upon one's subject,
they are called samyama.

Through mastery of samyama
comes the light of knowledge.

— PATANJALI'S YOGA SUTRAS

Samyama

By making samyama on
friendliness, compassion, etc.,
one develops the power of these qualities.

By making samyama on any kind of strength,
such as that of the elephant,
one obtains that strength.

By making samyama on the Inner Light,
one obtains knowledge of what is
subtle, hidden, or far distant.

By making samyama on the hollow of the throat,
one stills hunger and thirst.

By making samyama on the radiance
within the back of the head,
one becomes able to see the celestial beings.

All these powers of knowledge
may also come to one
whose mind is spontaneously
enlightened through purity.

— PATANJALI'S YOGA SUTRAS

The Pure Consciousness

ᕫᕬ.ᕫᕬ.ᕫᕬ.ᕫᕬ

The pure consciousness
of the Atman is unchangeable.
As the reflection of its consciousness
falls upon the mind,
the mind takes the form of the Atman,
and appears to be conscious.

The mind is able to perceive
because it reflects both the Atman
and the objects of perception.

Though the mind has innumerable
impressions and desires,
it acts only to serve the Atman;
being the compound substance,
it cannot act independently,
for its own sake.

The man of discrimination
ceases to regard the mind as the Atman.

— PATANJALI'S YOGA SUTRAS

Bhakti Is Intense Love for God

Now, therefore, we shall teach bhakti,
or the religion of divine love.

Bhakti is intense love for God.

In its intrinsic nature
this divine love is immortal bliss.

By attaining It,
a person becomes perfect,
immortal, and satisfied forever.

On attaining That
a man does not desire anything else;
he grieves no more,
is free from hatred or jealousy;
he does not take pleasure
in the vanities of life;
and he loses all eagerness
to gain anything for himself.

The devotee may first
become intoxicated with bliss.
Then, having realized That,
he becomes silent,
and takes his delight in the Atman.

— NARADA'S BHAKTI SUTRAS

WHOLE-SOULED DEVOTION

Bhakti cannot be used to fulfill any desire,
being itself the check to all desire.

Renunciation means
dedication of all activities,
secular as well as sacred,
to God.

A bhakta's renunciation means that
his whole soul goes toward God,
and whatever militates
against love for God
he rejects.

Whole-souled devotion means
giving up every other refuge,
and taking refuge in God.

To reject whatever militates
against love for God
means performance of such
secular and sacred activities
as are favorable to devotion to God.

— NARADA'S BHAKTI SUTRAS

THE CHARACTERISTICS OF DIVINE LOVE

The characteristics of divine love
have been described variously by sages
because of difference in their viewpoints.

Vyasa, son of Parasara, defines bhakti as
devotion to acts of worship and the like.

The sage Garga defines bhakti as
devotion to hearing and
praising the name of God.

The sage Shandilya defines bhakti as
avoiding all distracting thoughts, and
taking delight only in the Atman.

Narada gives these as the signs of bhakti:
When all thoughts, all words, and all deeds
are given up to the lord,
and when the least forgetfulness of God
makes one intensely miserable,
then love has begun.

Examples exist of
such perfect expressions of love.

— NARADA'S BHAKTI SUTRAS

UNTIL LOVE COMES

A man cannot be satisfied by the
knowledge or perception of God
until love comes.

Therefore, those who desire
to transcend all limitations and bondages
must accept supreme love
as the highest goal.

The great teachers describe,
in hymns and songs,
the following as the means of
attaining supreme love.

To attain supreme love,
a man must renounce
the objects of sense pleasure,
as well as attachment to them.

Supreme love is attained by
uninterrupted and constant
worship of God,
and by hearing of and singing
the glory of the Lord,
even while engaged in the
ordinary activities of life.

— NARADA'S BHAKTI SUTRAS

WHO OVERCOMES MAYA?

꧁·꧁·꧁·꧁

Who indeed overcomes maya?
He who gives up all attachment,
who serves the great ones,
and who is freed from the sense of
"I and Mine."

Who indeed overcomes maya?
He who gives up the fruits of his actions,
renounces all selfish activities,
and passes beyond the pairs of opposites.

Who indeed overcomes maya?
He who renounces even the
rites and ceremonies prescribed by the scriptures,
and attains unfaltering love for God.

Such a person, indeed, crosses this maya,
and helps others to cross it.

— NARADA'S BHAKTI SUTRAS

SUPREME LOVE

❦.❦.❦.❦

The real nature of this supreme love
is inexpressible.
Nevertheless, it is manifest in
the great souls who have attained it.

This supreme love is devoid of attributes;
it is free from all selfish desires;
it grows in intensity every moment;
it is an unbroken inner experience,
subtler than the subtlest.

When a man attains this supreme love,
he sees his Beloved everywhere,
he hears of Him everywhere,
he talks only of Him,
and he thinks of Him only.

— NARADA'S BHAKTI SUTRAS

GIVING UP THE FRUITS OF ACTION

The path of devotion
is the easiest way to attain God.
Love is its own proof
and does not require any other.
Its nature is peace and supreme bliss.

The devotee does not grieve at any personal loss,
for he has surrendered himself,
everything he has,
and even the rites and ceremonies
which are enjoined by the scriptures.

Even though the devotee may have
surrendered himself utterly to the Lord,
he must not renounce action in the world,
but continue to perform it,
giving up the fruits of action to the Lord.

— NARADA'S BHAKTI SUTRAS

FOR LOVE'S SAKE ONLY
෩·෩·෩·෩

Dedicate all your actions to God,
and direct all your passions,
such as lust, anger, pride, and so forth,
toward God.

Transcending the three forms of love,
love the Lord, and love Him as
His eternal servant, as His eternal bride.

The highest class of devotees are those
who have one-pointed love for God,
and for love's sake only.

When devotees talk of God,
their voices choke,
tears flow from their eyes,
and their hair stands erect
in ecstasy.

Such devotees as these
purify not only their families,
but this whole earth on which they are born.

— NARADA'S BHAKTI SUTRAS

Lovers of God

꩜.꩜.꩜.꩜

These great illumined souls,
the lovers of God,
sanctify the places of pilgrimage.
The deeds they perform become
examples of good action.

They give spiritual authority
to the scriptures.

Every one of those devotees has become
filled with the spirit of God.

When such lovers of God dwell on earth,
their forbearers rejoice, the gods dance in joy,
and this earth becomes sanctified.

Among them there are no distinctions
based on caste, learning, beauty of form,
birth in a high or low family,
wealth, possessions, and the like,
because they are His own.

— NARADA'S BHAKTI SUTRAS

THE GREATEST LOVE

While you study the devotional scriptures,
meditate upon their teachings and follow them
so that devotion to God
may be intensified in your heart.

It behooves a bhakta
not to waste a single moment,
nor to delay worshipping God until he
becomes freed from pleasure and pain,
from cravings and greed.

The bhakta should cultivate harmlessness,
truthfulness, purity, compassion,
faith, and other such virtues.

The blessed Lord alone
is to be worshipped day and night,
in and through every aspect of life
without any distracting thought.

Where the Lord is worshipped thus,
he soon reveals himself to the
inner vision of his devotees.

To love the eternal Truth —
this indeed is the greatest love.

— NARADA'S BHAKTI SUTRAS

THE SUPREME GOAL OF LIFE

A devotee loves to chant the praises
and glories of the blessed Lord.
A devotee loves His enchanting beauty.
A devotee loves to offer Him the worship of his heart.
A devotee loves to meditate on His presence constantly.
A devotee loves to think of himself as His servant.

A devotee loves Him as his friend.
A devotee loves Him as his child.
A devotee loves Him as his beloved.

A devotee loves to surrender himself to Him completely.
A devotee loves to be completely absorbed in Him.

Whosoever believes in
this auspicious description
of divine love by Narada,
and has faith in these teachings,
becomes a lover of God,
attains the highest beatitude,
and reaches the supreme goal of life.

— NARADA'S BHAKTI SUTRAS

THAT TRUTH SUPREME

꩜.꩜.꩜.꩜

He from whom the
creation, sustenance, and dissolution
of the universe take place;
who is both the material
and the instrumental cause of it;
who is omniscient;
who illumined the mind of Brahma
with the Vedic revelations;
in whom the worlds subsist in reality;
in whose light of consciousness
there is no place for anything false —
on that Truth Supreme we meditate.

— SRIMAD BHAGAVATAM

Spontaneous Devotion

๑๑.๑๑.๑๑.๑๑

It is true that sages
who are absorbed in the Self
are free from all bondages.
But they are endowed
with spontaneous devotion,
motivated by no self-centered desire.

Such is the inherent
attractiveness of the Lord,
that even such contemplatives,
steeped in Atman-consciousness,
are drawn to him.

— SRIMAD BHAGAVATAM

Unshakeable Love for the Lord

∽.∽.∽.∽

Krishna, the friend of devotees,
purifies the heart of those who take his name.
He manifests in the hearts of those
who hear the accounts of his deeds,
and erases all the evil tendencies
blocking their spiritual development.

When the obstructing evil tendencies
are mitigated,
through constant application to
the service of holy men and women,
and the study of holy Scriptures,
one develops a steady and unshakable love
for the Lord of abounding glory and grace.

—— SRIMAD BHAGAVATAM

THE SUPREME BEING AS AN ABSOLUTE REALITY

In the aspirant who has,
through the practice of devotion,
attained to purity, poise of mind,
and freedom from every form
of worldly attachments,
is generated the realization of
the Supreme Being
as an absolute Reality.

When the Supreme Soul
is thus realized within oneself,
the knots of the heart that
make one feel oneself as an ego
are severed;
the doubts of the mind
are dispelled;
and all the accumulated
karmas of the past,
as well as those in the offing,
are liquidated.

— SRIMAD BHAGAVATAM

ONE ULTIMATE TRUTH

Among the different and contradictory views
of the One Ultimate Truth
that are particularly upheld in systems
like Samkhya and Yoga;
that it is or that it is not,
that it has different characteristics
such as Personal or Impersonal,
there is no contradiction in reality,
for they all refer to, and are established in
the one and the same Infinite Supreme Reality.

— SRIMAD BHAGAVATAM

SALUTATIONS TO THE BLESSED ONE

෴.෴.෴.෴

OM,
salutations to the Blessed One,
whose presence makes the world
suffused with consciousness,
and who is the Self of all.
I meditate on that Supreme Lord,
the primordial source of all.

I take refuge in that
Self-existing Being,
in Whom is this universe,
from Whom is this universe,
by Whom is this universe,
who Himself is this universe
and who is also beyond this manifested universe
and the unmanifested Prakriti.

— SRIMAD BHAGAVATAM

Suffused with Happiness

✵ ✵ ✵ ✵

Never can desire be quenched
by repeated enjoyment of desires;
like butter poured on a fire
with a view to quenching it,
desire only gets inflamed thereby.

When a human being
does not have any
attitude of attachment
or hatred to any beings,
and remains always even-minded,
to that person,
all places always become
suffused with happiness.

— SRIMAD BHAGAVATAM

Our Salutations

Whom Brahma, Varuna, Indra, Rudra,
and Maruta praise in divine hymns,
whom the singers of Sama,
through the Vedas and the Upanishads,
praise in hymns,
whom the Yogis realize
with one-pointed mind
in the state of meditation,
and whose Infinite nature
all the devas and asuras do not perceive —
to that Divine Being be our salutations.

— SRIMAD BHAGAVATAM

ALL THAT WE ARE

All that we are is the result of what we have thought:
it is founded on our thoughts,
it is made up of our thoughts.
If a man speaks or acts with an evil thought,
pain follows him as the wheel follows
the foot of the ox that draws the carriage.

All that we are is the result of what we have thought:
it is founded on our thoughts,
it is made up of our thoughts.
If a man speaks or acts with a pure thought,
happiness follows him
like a shadow that never leaves him.

"He abused me, he beat me,
he defeated me, he robbed me," —
in those who harbor such thoughts
hatred will never cease.

"He abused me, he beat me,
he defeated me, he robbed me," —
in those who do not harbor such thoughts
hatred will cease.

For hatred does not cease by hatred at any time;
hatred ceases by love; this is an old rule.

— DHAMMAPADA

ON THE GOOD PATH

The evil-doer mourns in this world,
and he mourns in the next;
he mourns in both.
He mourns and suffers when he sees
the evil of his own work.

The virtuous man delights in this world,
and he delights in the next;
he delights in both.
He delights and rejoices when he sees
the purity of his own work.

The evil-doer suffers in this world,
and he suffers in the next;
he suffers in both.
He suffers when he thinks
of the evil he has done;
he suffers more
when going on the evil path.

The virtuous man is happy in this world,
and he is happy in the next;
he is happy in both.
He is happy when he thinks
of the good he has done;
he is still more happy
when going on the good path.

— DHAMMAPADA

To Discover Our True Self

ℭ∽.ℭ∽.ℭ∽.ℭ∽

Each individual has his inborn nature, svabhava,
and to make it effective in his life is his sacred duty,
svadharma.
Each individual is a focus of the Supreme,
a fragment of the Divine.
His destiny is to bring out in his life
this divine possibility.

The one Spirit of the universe has produced
the multiplicity of souls in the world,
but the Divine is our essential nature,
the very truth of our being.
So long as our work is done
in accordance with our nature,
we are righteous,
and if we dedicate it to God,
our work becomes a means of spiritual perfection.

When the divine in the individual is completely
manifested,
he attains to the Eternal Imperishable.
The problem that human life sets to us
is to discover our true Self,
and live according to its truth.

—— SARVEPALLI RADHAKRISHNAN

THE SUPREME IS THE INMOST SELF

The Supreme is the inmost Self of our existence.
All life is a movement of the rhythm of His life,
and our powers and acts are all derived from Him.

If, in our ignorance, we forget this deepest truth,
the truth does not alter.
If we live consciously in His truth
we will surrender all actions to God,
and escape from our ego.
If we do not, even then,
the truth will eventually prevail.

Sooner or later,
we will yield to the purpose of God,
but in the meanwhile,
there is no compulsion.

The Supreme desires our free cooperation,
when beauty and goodness flow
without travail and effortlessly.
When we become transparent media
for the light of God,
He uses us for His work.

— SARVEPALLI RADHAKRISHNAN

God's Own Men and Women

୭.୭.୭.୭

When we see the One Self in all things,
then equal-mindedness,
freedom from selfish desires,
surrender of our whole nature
to the Indwelling Spirit,
and love for all arise.

When these qualities are manifested,
our devotion is perfect,
and we are God's own men and women.

Our life then is guided not by the forces of
attraction and repulsion,
friendship and enmity,
pleasure and pain,
but by the single urge to give oneself to God,
and therefore to the service of the world,
which is one with God.

— SARVEPALLI RADHAKRISHNAN

You Are the Infinite Spirit

All these small ideas that
I am a man or a woman,
sick or healthy, strong or weak,
or that I hate or love or have little power,
are but hallucinations.

Stand up then!
Know that every thought and word
that weakens you in this world
is the only evil that exists.
Stand as a rock; you are the Infinite Spirit.
Say, "I am Existence Absolute,
Bliss Absolute, Knowledge Absolute,"
and like a lion breaking its cage,
break your chains and be free forever.

What frightens you, what holds you down?
Only ignorance of your true nature,
of your blessedness; nothing else can bind you.
You are the Pure One, the Ever-Blessed.

Therefore, if you dare, stand on that —
mold your whole life on that.
You are one with the Eternal Soul.
Know then that thou art He,
and model your whole life accordingly;
for those who know this
and model their lives accordingly,
will no more suffer in darkness.

— SWAMI VIVEKANANDA

The Glory of Our Own Soul

Vedanta teaches people
to have faith in themselves first.

As certain religions of the world say
that a person who does not believe
in a Personal God outside himself
is an atheist,
so Vedanta says that a person
who does not believe
in the God within himself
is an atheist.

Not believing in the glory of our own soul
is what Vedanta calls atheism.

—— SWAMI VIVEKANANDA

I WORSHIP HIM AS YOU

Vedanta says at every point,
"My friend, He whom you are
worshipping as unknown,
I worship Him as you.
He whom you are seeking
throughout the universe,
has been with you all the time.
You are living through Him,
for He is the Eternal Witness."

He is ever present as the eternal "I" —
He existing, the whole universe exists.
He is the light and life of the universe.
If this "I" were not in you, you could not see;
He shining through you, you see the world.

— SWAMI VIVEKANANDA

Children of Immortal Bliss

"Children of Immortal Bliss" —
what a sweet, what a hopeful name!
Allow me to call you, brethren,
by that sweet name —
"heirs of Immortal Bliss."

Yea, the Hindu refuses to call you sinners.
We are the children of God,
the sharers of Immortal Bliss,
holy and perfect beings.
Ye divinities on earth — sinners?
It is a sin to call a man so!
It is a standing libel on human nature!

Come up, O lions, and shake off the
delusion that you are sheep;
you are souls immortal,
spirits free, blest and eternal;
ye are not matter, ye are not bodies;
matter is your servant,
not you the servant of matter.

— SWAMI VIVEKANANDA

THE DOCTRINE OF LOVE

The Vedas proclaim
not an endless prison of cause and effect,
but the glorious truth that,
at the head of all natural laws,
and in and as every particle
of matter and force,
stands the One Infinite Existence.

And what is His nature?
He is everywhere,
the pure and formless One,
the Almighty and All-Merciful.

"Thou art our Father,
Thou art our Mother,
Thou art our beloved Friend,
Thou art the source of all strength."
Thus sang the rishis of the Vedas.

And how are we to worship Him?
Through love.

"He is to be worshipped as the one Beloved,
dearer than everything in this and the next life."
This is the doctrine of love declared in the Vedas.

— SWAMI VIVEKANANDA

Universal Religion

· ᘓᘐ.ᘓᘐ.ᘓᘐ.ᘓᘐ

If there is ever to be a universal religion,
it must be one that will have
no location in place or time,
one that will be infinite,
like the God it will preach;
one whose sun will shine upon
the followers of Krishna and of Christ,
on saints and sinners alike;
one that will not be Hindu or Buddhist,
Christian or Mohammedan,
but the sum total of all these,
with infinite space for development;
and one that with its catholicity
will embrace in its infinite arms
every human being,
from the lowest to the highest man.

It will be a religion that will have no place
for persecution or intolerance in its polity,
that will recognize divinity in every man and woman,
and whose whole scope, whose whole force,
will be centered in aiding humanity
to realize its own true, divine nature.

— SWAMI VIVEKANANDA

GOD ALONE REMAINS

Renunciation is the ideal preached by
all the great Prophets of the world.
What is meant by renunciation?
Unselfishness.
That is the only ideal in morality;
perfect unselfishness.

Here is the ideal:
when a man has
no more of his little self in him,
no possessor, nothing to call "me" or "mine,"
when a man has given up that little self to God,
destroyed his selfishness —
in that man God is manifest;
for in him, all selfish will is gone,
crushed out, annihilated.

That is the ideal.
We cannot reach that state yet;
nevertheless, let us worship the ideal,
and slowly struggle to reach it,
though it may be with faltering steps.
It may be tomorrow,
or it may be a thousand years hence,
but that ideal has to be reached,
for it is not only the end,
but also the means.
To be unselfish, perfectly selfless,
is salvation itself,
for the little self within dies,
and God alone remains.

— SWAMI VIVEKANANDA

I AM BRAHMAN

〜.〜.〜.〜

"The Atman has first to be heard of,
then reasoned upon, and then meditated upon."
This is the method of the Advaita Jnani.
The truth has to be heard, then reflected upon,
and then constantly asserted.

Think always,
"I am Brahman, I am the Infinite Spirit."
Every lesser thought must be
cast aside as weakening.
Cast aside every thought that says that
you are merely men or women.
Let body go, and let mind go:
let everything go but that One Existence.

"I am Brahman."
This is to be heard day after day.
Everything lesser must be thrown aside;
this truth is to be repeated continually, day and night,
poured through the ears until it reaches the heart;
until every nerve and muscle, and every drop of blood
tingles with the idea that "I am He, I am He."
It is the greatest strength; it is religion.
These are the words that will burn up
the dross that is in the mind,
words that will bring out the tremendous
energy which is within you already,
words that will awaken
the Infinite Power
which is sleeping in your heart.

— SWAMI VIVEKANANDA

The Oneness of Everything

Until we see nothing in the world
but the Lord Himself,
evils will beset us,
and we shall continue to make distinctions;
for it is only in the Lord, in the Spirit,
that we are all one,
and until we see God everywhere,
this unity will not exist for us.

Let us come to that consciousness
of the oneness of everything,
and let us see ourselves in everything.

Let us be no more worshippers
with small, limited notions of God,
but see Him in and as
everything in the universe.

Get rid of all these limited ideas
and see God in every person —
working through all hands,
walking through all feet,
and eating through every mouth.

In every being He lives,
through all minds He thinks.
To know this is religion.
When we feel this oneness,
we shall be free.

— SWAMI VIVEKANANDA

VIVEKA

To be able to use what we call viveka, discrimination,
to learn how, in every moment of our lives,
in every one of our actions, to discriminate between
right and wrong and true and false,
we will have to know the test of truth, which is purity, oneness.

Everything that makes for oneness is truth.
Love is truth, because it makes for oneness;
but ill-will is false, because ill-will in any form
makes for multiplicity.

It is ill-will that separates people;
therefore it is wrong and false.
It is a disintegrating power; it separates and destroys.
Love unites; love makes for that oneness,
for love is Existence, God Himself,
and all we see is the manifestation of that One Love,
more or less expressed.
The differences are only of degree;
it is the manifestation of that One Love throughout.

Therefore, in all our actions,
we have to judge whether or not
our act is making for oneness.
If it isn't, we have to give it up;
but if it is, we may be sure it is good.
So with our thoughts; we have to decide whether or not
they make for oneness, binding soul to soul,
and thus generating a great force.
If they do this, we will take them up,
and if not, we will throw them off as false
and harmful to our spiritual growth.

— SWAMI VIVEKANANDA

THE VOICE OF OUR HIGHER SELF

The goal of all religions is the same,
but the language of the teachers differs.
The goal is to destroy the selfish "I,"
so that the real "I," the Lord,
will reign through us.

We must cherish God alone.
We must say, "Not I, but Thou";
not my little personality
or any of its selfish clingings,
but He, and He alone, should reign.

"Thy will be done" — every moment
the traitor mind rebels against it;
yet we must say it again and again,
if we are ever to conquer the lower self.
We cannot serve a traitor and be free.

There is salvation for all
except for the traitor mind,
who must be destroyed.
We stand against our own Spirit,
against the majesty of God,
whenever we refuse to obey
the voice of our Higher Self.

— SWAMI VIVEKANANDA

The Sacrifice of the Little Self

Whatever good work we may do,
let us not claim any praise for it.
It is the Lord's; give up the fruits unto Him.

Let us stand aside and think that
we are only servants serving God,
and that every impulse for action
comes from Him every moment.

Whatever worship you offer,
whatever you do —
give all unto Him, and be at rest.
Let us all be at perfect peace with ourselves
as we give up our selfishness
as an eternal sacrifice unto the Lord.

Instead of pouring offerings into the fire,
perform this one great sacrifice day and night —
the sacrifice of your little self.

— SWAMI VIVEKANANDA

THE MORE SHALL WE LOVE

We have to bear in mind that
we are all debtors to the world,
and that the world does not owe us anything.
It is a great privilege for all of us to be
allowed to do anything for the world.
In helping the world we truly help ourselves.

This world will always continue to be
a mixture of good and evil.
Our duty is to help
and sympathize with the weak,
and to love even the wrongdoer.

It is important to always keep in mind
that the world is for us a grand moral gymnasium,
wherein we are all blessed to be able to
take exercise in order to become
stronger and stronger spiritually.

The result of this exercise is that
the more selfless we become,
the more shall we love,
and the better will be our work.

— SWAMI VIVEKANANDA

STAND ASIDE AND LET GOD WORK

Our best work is done,
our greatest influence is exerted,
when we are without thought of self.
All great geniuses know this.
Let us open ourselves to the one Divine Actor,
and let Him act through us.

Be perfectly unfocused upon yourself;
then alone will you do true work.
Put out self, lose it, forget it;
just let God work through you;
it is His business.

We have nothing to do but
stand aside and let God work.
The more we go away,
the more God comes in.
Get rid of the little "I," and
let only the great "I" live through you.

— SWAMI VIVEKANANDA

CONQUER YOURSELF

෨෨.෨෨.෨෨.෨෨

We are what our thoughts have made us;
so take care of what you think.
Thoughts live; they travel far.
Desire nothing selfishly;
give, think of God,
and look for no return.
It is the selfless who bring results.

The Lord has hidden Himself best,
and His work is best;
so he who hides himself best,
accomplishes most.
Conquer yourself,
and the whole universe is yours.

— SWAMI VIVEKANANDA

BHAKTI YOGA

Bhakti yoga is the science of higher love.
It shows us how to direct love:
how to manage it, how to use it,
how to give it a new aim;
and from it, it shows us how to obtain
the highest and most glorious results;
that is, how to make it lead us
to spiritual blessedness.

Bhakti yoga does not say, "Give up";
it only says, "Love the Highest!"
and everything low
will naturally fall away from him,
the object of whose love
is this Highest.

What is really required of us in this yoga
is that our thirst after the beautiful
should be directed to God.

What is the beauty in the human face,
in the sky, in the stars, and in the moon?
It is only the partial manifestation of the real,
all-embracing Divine Beauty.
"He shining, everything shines."

— SWAMI VIVEKANANDA

LOVE, LOVER, AND THE BELOVED ARE ONE

We all have to begin as dualists
in the religion of love.
God is to us a separate Being,
and we feel ourselves to be separate beings also.

Love then comes in the middle,
and we begin to approach God,
and God also comes nearer and nearer to us.
We take up all the various relationships of life,
as son or daughter, as mother or father,
as friend, as lover, and so on,
and we project them on our ideal of love,
on our God.
To us, God exists as all these,
and the last point of our progress is reached
when we become absolutely merged
with the object of our worship.

We all begin with love for ourselves,
and the unfair claims of the little self
make even love selfish.
At last, however, comes the full blaze of light,
in which this little self is seen to have become
one with the Infinite.
We ourselves are transfigured
in the presence of this Light of Love,
and we realize at last the
beautiful and inspiring truth
that Love, the Lover, and the Beloved,
are One.

— SWAMI VIVEKANANDA

APPROACHING THE CENTER

There may be millions of radii
converging toward the same center in the sun.
The farther they are from the center,
the greater is the distance between any two.
But as they all meet at the center,
all difference vanishes.

There is such a center,
which is the absolute goal of humankind.
It is God.
We are the radii.
The distances between the radii are the
constitutional limitations through which
we alone can catch the vision of God.
While standing on this plane,
each one of us is bound to have a
different view of the Absolute Reality;
and as such, all views are true,
and not one of us need quarrel with another.

The only solution lies in approaching the center.
If we try to settle our differences by argument or quarreling,
we shall find that we can go on for thousands of years,
without coming to a conclusion.
History proves that.

The only solution is to march ahead toward the center,
toward God, and the sooner we do that,
the sooner our differences will vanish.

— SWAMI VIVEKANANDA

NOT I, BUT THOU

୬ର.୬ର.୬ର.୬ର

What is knowledge?
And what is the nature of this ego?
God alone is the doer, and none else —
that is knowledge.

I am not the doer;
I am a mere instrument in his hand.

Therefore I say,
"O Mother, Thou art the operator,
and I am the machine.
Thou art the indweller,
and I am the house.
Thou art the driver,
and I am the carriage.

"I move as Thou movest me.
I do as Thou makest me do.
I speak as Thou makest me speak.
Not I, not I, but Thou, but Thou."

— SRI RAMAKRISHNA

ALL PATHS LEAD TO TRUTH

The devotee coming down from samadhi
perceives that it is Brahman that has become
the ego, the universe, and all living beings.
This is known as the Vijnana.
This path of knowledge leads to Truth,
as does the path that combines
knowledge and love.

The path of love, too,
leads to this goal.
The way of love is as true
as the way of knowledge.
All paths ultimately lead
to the same Truth.

But as long as God keeps
the feeling of ego in us,
it is easier to follow the path of love.

— SRI RAMAKRISHNA

I Am Thy Servant

Why does a vijnani keep
an attitude of love toward God?
The answer is that "I-consciousness" persists.
It disappears in the state of samadhi, no doubt,
but it comes back.

In the case of ordinary people,
the "I" of ego never disappears.
You may cut down the tree,
but the next day sprouts shoot up.

Once Rama asked his faithful servant, Hanuman,
"How do you look on me?"
And Hanuman replied,
"O Rama, as long as I have the feeling of 'I,'
I see that Thou art the whole and I am a part,
that Thou art the master and I am thy servant.

"But when, O Rama, I have the knowledge of Truth,
then I realize that Thou art I, and I am Thou."

Since this "I" must remain,
let the rascal ego be God's servant.

— SRI RAMAKRISHNA

Thou Art the Master

⁕⁕⁕⁕

"I" and "mine" —
these constitute ignorance.
"My house," "my wealth,"
"my learning," "my possessions" —
the attitude that prompts one to say such things
comes from ignorance.

On the contrary,
the attitude born of Knowledge is,
"O God, Thou art the master,
and all these things belong to Thee.
House, family, children,
friends, all are Thine."

— SRI RAMAKRISHNA

ONE UNDER DIFFERENT NAMES

A lake has several ghats.
At one,
the Hindus take water in pitchers,
and call it "jal";
at another,
the Muslims take water in leather bags,
and call it "pani."
At a third, the Christians call it "water."
Can we imagine that it is not "jal,"
but only "pani" or "water"?

The substance is one under different names,
and everyone is seeking the same substance;
only climate, temperament, and name create differences.
Let each follow his own path.
If he sincerely and ardently
wishes to know God,
peace be unto him!
He will surely realize Him.

— SRI RAMAKRISHNA

His Names Are Many
∾.∾.∾.∾

Suppose a man has several sons.
The older boys address him distinctly
as "Baba" or "Papa,"
but the babies can at best
call him "Ba" or "Pa."

Now, will the father be angry
with those who address him
in this indistinct way?
The father knows that
they too are calling him,
only they cannot pronounce the name well.
All children are the same to the father.

Likewise, the devotees call on God alone,
though by different names.
They call on one God only.
God is one,
but His names are many.

—— SRI RAMAKRISHNA

THE JNANIS

He who is called Brahman by the jnanis
is known as Atman by the yogis
and as Bhagavan, Lord, by the bhaktas.
The same brahmin is called priest
when worshipping in the temple
and cook when preparing a meal in the kitchen.

The jnani, sticking to
the path of knowledge,
always reasons about the Reality,
saying, "Not this, not this."
Brahman is neither "this" nor "that";
It is neither the universe nor its living beings.
Reasoning in this way,
the mind becomes steady.
Then it disappears,
and the aspirant reaches samadhi.

This is the Knowledge of Brahman.
It is the unwavering conviction of the jnani
that Brahman alone is real,
and the world illusory.
All these names and forms are illusory,
like a dream.
What Brahman is cannot be described.
This is the opinion of the jnanis,
the followers of Vedanta philosophy.

— SRI RAMAKRISHNA

The Bhaktas

The bhaktas,
the lovers of the Personal God,
accept all the states of consciousness;
they take the waking state to be real also.

They don't think the world to be illusory,
like a dream.
They say that the universe is a manifestation
of God's power and glory.
God has created all these things —
sky, stars, moon, sun, mountains, ocean,
men and women, animals.
They constitute His glory.

He is within us, in our hearts.
And He is outside.
The most advanced devotees say that
He Himself has become all this —
the universe and all living beings —
while the devotee of God
wants to taste the sugar,
not be the sugar.

— SRI RAMAKRISHNA

The Reality Is One

The Primordial Power is ever at play.
She is creating, preserving, and destroying,
in play, as it were.
This Power is called Shakti.
Shakti is verily Brahman, and
Brahman is verily Shakti.
It is one and the same Reality.

When we think of It as inactive,
that is to say, not engaged in the acts of
creation, preservation, and destruction,
then we call It Brahman.

But when It engages in these activities,
then we call it Shakti.
The Reality is one and the same;
the difference is in name and form.

— SRI RAMAKRISHNA

PURE LOVE FOR THEE

ରେ . ରେ . ରେ . ରେ

To my Divine Mother,
I prayed only for pure love.
I offered flowers at Her Lotus Feet,
and prayed to Her,

"Mother,
here is Thy virtue, here is Thy vice.
Take them both, and
grant me only pure love for Thee.

"Here is Thy knowledge,
here is Thy ignorance.
Take them both, and
grant me only pure love for Thee.

"Here is Thy purity,
here is Thy impurity.
Take them both, Mother, and
grant me only pure love for Thee.

"Here is Thy dharma,
here is Thy adharma.
Take them both, Mother, and
grant me only pure love for Thee."

— SRI RAMAKRISHNA

GOD IS THE DOER

There is only one Guru,
and that is Satchidananda.
He alone is the Teacher.
My attitude toward God is that of
a child toward its mother.
One can get human gurus by the million.
All want to be teachers.
But who cares to be a disciple?

Without a commission from God,
a man becomes vain.
He says to himself, "I am teaching people."
This vanity comes from ignorance,
for only an ignorant person feels that he is the doer.

A man verily becomes liberated in life if he feels,
"God is the Doer. He alone is doing everything.
I am doing nothing."

Man's sufferings and worries
spring only from his persistent thought
that he is the doer.

— SRI RAMAKRISHNA

The Reality Is One and the Same

Do you know how a lover of God feels?
His attitude is,
"O God, Thou are the Master, and I am Thy servant."
"Thou art the Mother, and I am Thy child."
Or again,
"Thou are my Father and Mother."
"Thou art the Whole, and I am a part."
The bhakta doesn't like to say,
"I am Brahman."

The yogi, however,
seeks to realize the Atman,
the Supreme Soul within.
His ideal is the union of the embodied soul
and the Supreme Soul.
He withdraws his mind from sense-objects,
and tries to concentrate it on the Atman.

But the Reality is one and the same.
The difference is only in name.
He who is Brahman, the Infinite One,
is verily Atman, the Indwelling Soul,
and again, He is also the Bhagavan, Lord,
the Personal God of the bhakta.

He is Brahman to the
followers of the path of knowledge,
Atman to the yogis,
and Lord to the lovers of God.

— SRI RAMAKRISHNA

The Salt Doll

Once a salt doll went to measure
the depth of the ocean.
No sooner was it in the water,
than it melted.
Now who was left to tell the depth?

There is a sign
of Perfect Knowledge.
The seeker becomes silent
when It is attained.

Then the "I,"
which may be likened to the salt doll,
melts in the Ocean of
Existence-Knowledge-Bliss Absolute,
and becomes one with It.
Not the slightest trace of distinction is left.

— SRI RAMAKRISHNA

THE CHAMELEON

A devotee thinks of God as he sees Him.
Once a man entered a wood and saw a small animal on a tree.
He came back and told another man that he had seen a creature
of a beautiful red color on a certain tree.

The second man replied: "When I went into the wood,
I also saw the animal. But why do you call it red? It is green.
Another man who was present contradicted them both,
insisting that it was yellow. Presently others arrived
saying that it was gray, violet, blue, and so on.
At last they started quarreling among themselves.

To settle the dispute they all went to the tree.
They saw a man sitting under it. On being asked, he replied;
"Yes, I live under this tree and I know the animal very well.
All your descriptions are true.
Sometimes it appears red, sometimes yellow,
and at other times blue, violet, gray, and so forth.
It is a chameleon. And sometimes it has no color at all."

In like manner, only one who constantly thinks of God
can know His real nature; he alone knows that
God reveals Himself to seekers in various forms and aspects.
God has attributes; then again He has none.

Only the man who lives under the tree knows that the chameleon
can appear in various colors, and, at times, with no color at all.
It is the others who suffer from the agony of futile argument.

Kabir used to say, "The formless Absolute is my Father,
and God with form is my Mother." God reveals Himself
in the form which His devotee loves most.

—— SRI RAMAKRISHNA

154

THE LOTUS FEET OF GOD

In the light of Vedantic reasoning,
Brahman has no attributes;
the real nature of Brahman cannot be described.
But so long as your individuality is real to you,
the world also is real,
and equally real are the different forms of God,
and the feeling that God is a Person.

Yours is the path of bhakti.
That is very good; it is an easy path.
Who can fully know the infinite God?
And what need is there of knowing the Infinite?
Having attained this rare human birth,
the supreme need is to develop love
for the Lotus Feet of God.

— SRI RAMAKRISHNA

THE ELEPHANT

Once some blind men chanced to come near an animal
that someone told them was an elephant.
They were asked what the elephant was like.
The blind men began to feel its body.

One of them said the elephant was like a pillar;
he had touched only its leg.
Another said it was like a winnowing-fan;
he had touched only its ear.

In this way the others, having touched its tail or belly,
gave their different versions of the elephant.
Just so, a man who has seen only one aspect of God,
limits God to that alone.
It is his conviction that God cannot be anything else.

How can you say that the
only truth about God is that He has form?

It is undoubtedly true that
God comes down to earth in a human form,
as in the case of Krishna.
And it is true as well that God reveals Himself
to His devotees in various forms.

But it is also true that God is formless,
the Indivisible Existence-Knowledge-Bliss Absolute.

— SRI RAMAKRISHNA

BEYOND VIRTUE AND VICE

Those whose spiritual consciousness has been awakened,
who have realized that God alone is real,
and all else illusory, cherish a different ideal.
They are aware that God alone is the Doer,
and all are His instruments.

Those whose spiritual consciousness has been awakened
never make a false step.
They do not have to reason in order to shun evil.
They are so full of love of God that
whatever action they undertake is a good action.
They are fully conscious that
they are not the doers of their actions,
but mere servants of God.
They always feel,
"I am the machine and He is the Operator.
I do as He does through me.
I speak as He speaks through me.
I move as He moves me."

Fully awakened souls
are beyond virtue and vice.
They realize that it is God
who does everything.

— SRI RAMAKRISHNA

To Enjoy Its Own Bliss

The whole thing is to love God
and taste His sweetness.
He is sweetness and the devotee is its enjoyer.
The devotee drinks the sweet Bliss of God.
God is the lotus and the devotee the bee.
The devotee sips the honey of the lotus.

As a devotee cannot live without God,
so also God cannot live without His devotee.
Then the devotee becomes the sweetness,
and God its enjoyer.
The devotee becomes the lotus, and God the bee.
It is the Godhead that has become these two
in order to enjoy Its own Bliss.

— SRI RAMAKRISHNA

TRUTH

⁖⁖⁖⁖

It is said that truthfulness alone
constitutes the spiritual discipline of the Kaliyuga.
If a man clings tenaciously to truth,
he ultimately realizes God.
Without this regard for truth,
one gradually loses everything.

If by chance I say that I will go to the pine-grove,
I must go there even if there is no further need of it,
lest I lose my attachment to truth.

After my vision of the Divine Mother,
I prayed to Her, taking a flower in my hands,

"Mother, here is Thy knowledge and here is Thy ignorance.
Take them both, and give me only pure love.
Here is Thy holiness and here is Thy unholiness.
Take them both, Mother, and give me pure love.
Here is Thy good and here is Thy evil.
Take them both, Mother, and give me pure love.
Here is Thy righteousness and here is Thy unrighteousness.
Take them both, Mother, and give me pure love."
I mentioned all these, but I could not say,
"Mother, here is Thy truth and here is Thy falsehood.
Take them both."
I gave up everything at Her feet,
but could not bring myself to give up truth.

— SRI RAMAKRISHNA

THE SAME LORD WITH A THOUSAND NAMES

I have practiced
Hinduism, Islam, Christianity —
and I have also followed the paths
of the different Hindu sects.
I have found that it is the same God
toward whom all are directing their steps,
though along different paths.

You should try all beliefs
and traverse all different ways once.

Wherever I look,
I see people quarreling
in the name of religion.
But they never reflect that
He who is called Krishna
is also called Shiva
and bears the name of Primal Energy,
Mother, Jesus, and Allah as well —
the same Lord, with a thousand names.

— SRI RAMAKRISHNA

GOD ALONE IS REAL

Discrimination is the reasoning by which
one knows that God alone is real,
and all else is unreal.
Real means eternal, and
unreal means impermanent.
He who has acquired discrimination
knows that God is the only Substance,
and all else is non-existent.
With the awakening of this
spirit of discrimination,
a man wants to know God.

On the contrary,
if a man loves the unreal —
such things as creature comforts,
name, fame, and wealth —
then he doesn't want to know God,
who is of the very nature of Reality.
It is through discrimination between
the Real and the unreal that
one seeks to know God.

— SRI RAMAKRISHNA

The Power of the Divine Mother

The Divine Mother revealed to me
in the Kali temple
that it was She
who had become everything.

She showed me
that everything was full of Consciousness:
the image was Consciousness,
the altar was Consciousness,
the water vessels were Consciousness,
the doorsill was Consciousness,
the marble floor was Consciousness —
all was Consciousness.

I found everything inside the room soaked,
as it were, in Bliss — the Bliss of Satchidananda.
I saw a wicked man in front of the Kali temple;
but even in him I saw
the Power of the Divine Mother vibrating.

— SRI RAMAKRISHNA

Tears of Devotion

ᏍᎤ.ᏍᎤ.ᏍᎤ.ᏍᎤ

DEVOTEE
"Sir, to see you is the same as to see God."

SRI RAMAKRISHNA
"Don't ever say that again.
The waves belong to the Ganges,
not the Ganges to the waves.
A man cannot realize God
unless he gets rid of
all such egotistic ideas as
'I am such an important man'
or 'I am so and so.'
Level the mound of 'I' to the ground
by dissolving it with tears of devotion."

— SRI RAMAKRISHNA

RESTLESS FOR GOD

∽∽.∽∽.∽∽.∽∽

DEVOTEE
"Why do we not feel
intense restlessness to realize God?"

SRI RAMAKRISHNA
"A man does not feel restless for God
until all his worldly desires are satisfied.
He does not remember the Mother of the Universe
until his share of enjoyment is completed.

"A child absorbed in play
does not seek his mother.
But after his play is over, he says,
'Mother! I must go to mother.'"

— SRI RAMAKRISHNA

ONE'S OWN SELF

∽.∽.∽.∽

According to the Vedanta,
one has to know the real nature
of one's own Self.
But such knowledge is impossible
without the renunciation of ego.

The ego is like a stick that
seems to divide the water in two.
It makes you feel that you are one
and I am another.
When the ego disappears in samadhi,
then one knows Brahman to be
one's own inner consciousness.

— SRI RAMAKRISHNA

EVERYTHING IS ITS MANIFESTATION

At first one discriminates,
"Not this, not this," and feels that
God alone is real and all else is illusory.
Afterward the same person finds that
it is God Himself who has become all this —
the universe, maya, and the living beings.
First negation, and then affirmation.

This is the view held by the Puranas.
Just so, one can attain Satchidananda
by negating the universe and its living beings.
But after the attainment of Satchidananda,
one finds that Satchidananda Itself
has become the universe and all living beings.

Everything is possible for God.
First of all reach the indivisible Satchidananda,
and then, coming down, look at the universe.
You will then find that
everything is Its manifestation.
It is God alone who has become everything.
The world by no means exists apart from Him.

— SRI RAMAKRISHNA

ALL PURE SPIRIT
୭୭.୭୭.୭୭.୭୭

I used to worship the Deity in the Kali temple.
It was suddenly revealed to me that
everything is Pure Spirit.
The utensils of worship, the altar, the doorframe —
all Pure Spirit.
People, animals, and other living beings —
all Pure Spirit.
Then, like a madman,
I began to shower flowers in all directions.
Whatever I saw I worshipped.

One day, while worshipping Shiva,
I was about to offer a bel leaf
on the head of the image,
when it was revealed to me that
this Universe Itself is Shiva.
After that, my worship of Shiva through the image
came to an end.

Another day I had been plucking flowers,
when it was revealed to me that
the flowering plants were so many bouquets.
It was revealed to me in a flash. I didn't calculate about it.
It was shown to me that each plant was a bouquet,
adorning the Universal Form of God.
That was the end of my plucking flowers.

I look on man in just the same way.
When I see a man, I see that it is God Himself
who walks on earth.

— SRI RAMAKRISHNA

OM Is Brahman

ᘒᘒ.ᘒᘒ.ᘒᘒ.ᘒᘒ

The sound OM is Brahman.
The rishis and sages
practiced austerity to
realize that Sound-Brahman.

After attaining perfection
one hears the sound of this eternal Word
rising spontaneously from the navel.

"What will you gain," some sages ask,
"by merely hearing this sound?"

You hear the roar of the ocean
from a distance.
By following the roar
you can reach the ocean.
As long as there is the roar,
there must also be the ocean.
By following the trail of OM
you attain Brahman,
of which the Word is the symbol.

— SRI RAMAKRISHNA

GLOSSARY

ADHARMA. Conduct contrary to one's sacred duty or righteous path and in opposition to divine law.

ADVAITA. Literally, "not two." The Vedanta school of non-dualism that teaches the Oneness of existence.

ANANDA. Absolute, undifferentiated Bliss, beyond the duality of pain and pleasure.

ASANA. Posture. The third of the eight steps of Raja yoga.

ASURAS. Power-seeking deities in Hindu mythology, opposed to and constantly competing with the Devas.

ATMAN. The Supreme Soul; the One Existence indwelling; the Self. *Atman* is used interchangeably with *Brahman* in referring to the One Ultimate Existence.

BHAGAVAD GITA. The revered Hindu scripture in which Lord Krishna teaches Arjuna the great spiritual truths and yoga pathways to union with God.

BHAGAVAN. Lord, with specific reference to one of Brahman's divine forms with personality and attributes. A title of veneration to a personal God, as in "Bhagavan Shiva," or "Bhagavan Krishna."

BHAKTA. A follower of Bhakti yoga; a devotee of a Personal God.

BHAKTI YOGA. One of the four classical yogas. The path of union through devotion to and love of a Personal God.

BRAHMAN. The One Infinite Existence of the non-dualistic Advaita Vedanta philosophy; Satchidananda, Existence, Consciousness, and Bliss Absolute. The One Reality.

CHIT. Absolute, undifferentiated Consciousness. Also referred to as Infinite Knowledge.

DEVAS. Benevolent divine beings or gods in Hindu mythological texts.

DHARANA. The sixth of the eight steps of Raja yoga, meaning concentration, the fixing of the mind on one point alone, to the exclusion of all else.

DHARMA. One's sacred duty, righteous path, or virtuous conduct in conformity with the principle of cosmic order and divine law.

DHYANA. The seventh of the eight steps of Raja yoga, meaning meditation, the unbroken contemplation of the object of concentration.

GITA. See Bhagavad Gita.

GUNAS. The three qualities, or energies, that make up everything in the material universe: tamas, inertia and ignorance; rajas, activity and passion; and sattva, purity and illumination.

GURU. Literally, "slayer of darkness"; a spiritual teacher and guide.

IMPERSONAL GOD. The One Infinite Existence. Brahman, the One Absolute Reality beyond qualities or form.

ISHWARA. The Personal God. The greatest manifestation of impersonal Brahman possible within the limitations of time, space, and causation. The supreme Creator, Sustainer, and Dissolver of the Universe.

JNANA YOGA. One of the four classical yogas. The path of union with God through knowledge and intellectual discrimination.

JNANI. A follower of Jnana yoga.

KARMA. Action or work; but within Vedanta philosophy, Karma chiefly refers to the effects or consequences of actions or work.

KRISHNA. The Incarnation of God that teaches the great spiritual truths and yoga pathways to Arjuna in the Bhagavad Gita.

MAHAVAKYAS. The great affirmations of truth found in the Upanishads.

MANTRA. The name of God given to a disciple from his or her spiritual teacher during initiation. Also, a holy word, verse, or hymn from the Vedas.

MAYA. The illusion of name and form that hides the underlying Unity of Existence.

MOKSHA. Sanskrit for "liberation," the final freeing of the individual soul from the bondage of all egoism (selfishness), allowing for the ultimate bliss of union with the Infinite Soul, or Atman.

NARADA. A saint in Hindu mythology.

NIYAMA. The second of the eight steps of Raja yoga, made up of five observances, or virtues, that the devotee is called on to practice and perfect.

OM. The most sacred word of the Vedas. It is the symbol both of the Personal God and of the Absolute.

PATANJALI. The author of the Yoga Sutras, the scripture of Raja yoga.

PERSONAL GOD. God with attributes and qualities.

PRAKRITI. Undifferentiated nature, from which all things material arise, consisting of the three gunas: sattva, rajas, and tamas.

PRANA. The primal energy. The essential substrate of all forms of energy. The infinite, omnipresent manifesting power of this universe.

PRATYAHARA. The discipline of withdrawing the mind and internal sense organs from external sense objects; the fifth of the eight steps of Raja yoga.

PURANAS. Hindu religious texts telling the stories of deities, kings, heroes, and demigods.

RAJAS. One of the three primal qualities, or energies, that make up nature; the force of activity and passion. See Gunas.

RAJA YOGA. One of the four classical yogas, taught by Patanjali in his Yoga Sutras.

RAJA YOGI. A devotee who follows the practices of Raja yoga.

RAMA. One of the most widely worshipped and beloved Hindu deities.

RIG VEDA. One of the four Vedas. See Vedas.

RISHI. A seer of Truth; a sage.

SAMADHI. The superconscious state in which the ultimate union with God is achieved.

SAMSKARA. Mental impressions, created through thoughts or actions, that become tendencies through repetition and, over time, harden into the habits that make up character.

SAMYAMA. The practice of the last three steps of Raja yoga, one following the other, on a particular object of contemplation. Concentration (dharana), meditation (dhyana), and absorption (samadhi).

SAMKHYA. One of the six systems of orthodox Hindu philosophy.

SAT. Absolute, undifferentiated Existence. Also referred to as Infinite Being.

SATCHIDANANDA. Also Sat-Chit-Ananda. Existence, Consciousness, and Bliss Absolute. According to the Vedanta philosophy,

Satchidananda is the highest concept of God possible to the mind.

SATTVA. One of the three primal qualities, or energies, that make up nature; sattva is the quality of purity, goodness, and illumination. See Gunas.

SELF. The same as Brahman, or the Infinite Spirit.

self. The ego, the small sense of "I."

SELF-REALIZATION. The supreme goal in life, the attainment of Unity with the Infinite Soul, or Atman.

SHAKTI. The active manifesting power of the universe, worshipped as God the Mother.

SOHAM. Literally, "I am He." A mantra used by non-dualists to remind themselves that they are One with Brahman.

SOUL. The same as Brahman, or the Infinite Spirit.

soul. The individual soul.

SRI. A prefix giving honor to the names of deities and eminent persons.

SWAMI. The title of a Hindu monk.

TAMAS. One of the three primal qualities, or energies, that make up nature; tamas is the quality of darkness, inertia, and ignorance. See Gunas.

UPANISHADS. The last revelations of the Vedas, where the Vedanta philosophy of Oneness is first and most beautifully proclaimed. There are 108 of them, of which eleven are regarded as major Upanishads.

VEDANTA. Literally, "the end," or "culmination," of the Vedas. A system of philosophy based on the teachings of the Upanishads, proclaiming the final reality of Brahman, the One Existence, manifested as all things in the universe.

VEDAS. The most sacred Hindu scriptures, consisting of four parts: the Rig, Sama, Yajur, and Atharva.

VIJNANA. The highest level of knowing. The absolute, intimate, and constant apprehension of God.

VIJNANI. A fully illumined soul who, after attaining illumination, strives for the illumination of others.

VIVEKA. Discrimination between the real and the unreal, between the One Infinite Existence and the temporary forms of the world.

YAMA. The first of the eight steps of Raja yoga, made up of five restraints, or disciplines, that the devotee is called on to practice and perfect.

YOGA. Union with God. Denotes the union of the individual soul with the Supreme Soul and the disciplines that lead to such union. The four classical pathways to union with God are Bhakti, Jnana, Karma, and Raja.

YOGI. One who practices yoga.

ACKNOWLEDGMENTS

My deepest thanks to:

Swami Swahananda, for his majestic and constant kindness, encouragement, and support.

Swami Sarvadevananda, for his continually inspiring example of love and spiritual light.

Shiva, for his unwavering support and invaluable assistance with this book.

Swami Prabhavananda and Swami Nikhilananda, two of the greatest spiritual teachers of the twentieth century, who played such great roles in opening my heart and mind to the blessings of India's sacred wisdom.

Vedanta Press and the Vedanta Society of Southern California for their generosity with excerpts from Swami Prabhavananda's *How to Know God* and *Narada's Way of Divine Love*, and for what is one of the finest and most comprehensive resources for Indian wisdom on the Internet, their outstanding online bookstore, www.vedanta.com.

The Blue Mountain Center of Meditation and Nilgiri Press, for their generosity with excerpts from Sri Easwaran's wonderful translations of the Upanishads and Bhagavad Gita.

Sri Eknath Easwaran, for having had such a great impact on my love and understanding of India's scriptural treasures. To learn more about the wealth of wisdom offered by this great spiritual teacher, visit www.easwaran.org.

Advaita Ashrama, for being so generous over the years with selections from so many of their wonderful books.

Huston Smith, for first opening my heart and mind to the glory of ancient India's Vedanta wisdom and yoga scriptures through his masterpiece, *The World's Religions*.

All the blessed souls of the Ramakrishna Order of India, who tirelessly continue to do so much to bring greater light and love to India and the world. My heart overflows with love for you.

SOURCES AND CREDITS

ASTAVAKRA SAMHITA. This great Vedanta scripture is presented in the form of a dialogue between the sage Astavakra and King Janaka. It offers a powerful and unapologetic presentation of the cardinal principles of Advaita, or strictly monistic Vedanta. All excerpts here are from the Astavakra Samhita, translated by Swami Nityaswarupananda, published by Advaita Ashrama, copyright 1998.

BHAGAVAD GITA. The most beloved yoga scripture in India, it is made up of the most ancient teachings on the classical yoga pathways to Oneness, given by Sri Krishna to his disciple Arjuna. All excerpts here are from *The Bhagavad Gita*, translated by Eknath Easwaran, founder of the Blue Mountain Center of Meditation, copyright 1985; reprinted by permission of Nilgiri Press, P.O. Box 256, Tomales, CA 94971, www.easwaran.org.

BHAKTI SUTRAS. One of the most revered devotional classics, the Bhakti Sutras present the main tenets of the religion of divine love through the teachings of the sage Narada. All excerpts here are from *Narada's Way of Divine Love*, copyright 1971, translated by Swami Prabhavananda; reprinted by permission of Vedanta Press, Hollywood, CA 90068, www.vedanta.com.

DHAMMAPADA. The oldest teachings of the Buddha, compiled after his death by his devotees.

RAMAKRISHNA (1836–1886). The revered Bengali saint whose great spiritual light ignited India's modern spiritual renaissance. Ramakrishna was the living embodiment of the truth in all religions and the glory of the divine love of the Mother. All excerpts here are from *The Gospel of Ramakrishna*, as translated by Swami Nikhilananda, copyright 1942 by the Ramakrishna-Vivekananda Center of New York.

SRIMAD BHAGAVATAM. One of the most important and beloved classical scriptures of India, it describes the life and times of Krishna. Its main focus is on the teachings of Bhakti yoga, or loving devotion to God.

UPANISHADS. The final teachings of the Vedas, the Upanishads are source wisdom for such sacred spiritual principles and practices as Oneness, the divinity of the soul, yoga, meditation, karma, rebirth, and spiritual psychology. All excerpts here are from *The Upanishads*, translated by Eknath Easwaran, founder of the Blue Mountain Center of Meditation, copyright 1985; reprinted by permission of Nilgiri Press, P.O. Box 256, Tomales, CA 94971, www.easwaran.org.

VIVEKANANDA. The first realized Indian master to teach yoga to the West, Vivekananda electrified the 1893 World Parliament of Religions and then spent years in America teaching the Vedanta principles of the Oneness of existence, the Divinity of the soul, and the truth in all religions. He is revered by millions of people in India as one of the greatest embodiments of human spiritual attainment and service.

YOGA SUTRAS. The Yoga Sutras of Patanjali is the bible of Raja yoga, the pathway to truth based on introspection, mind mastery, and meditation. All excerpts here are from *How to Know*

BOOKS RECOMMENDED
FOR FURTHER STUDY

Burke, Marie Louise. *Swami Vivekananda in the West: New Discoveries*. 3 vols. Calcutta: Advaita Ashrama, 1983–1985.

DeLuca, Dave, ed. *Pathways to Joy: The Master Vivekananda on the Four Yoga Paths to God*. Novato, CA: New World Library, 2006.

Easwaran, Eknath, trans. *The Bhagavad Gita*. Tomales, CA: Nilgiri Press, 1985.

———, trans. *The Upanishads*. Tomales, CA: Nilgiri Press, 1985.

His Eastern and Western Disciples. *The Life of Swami Vivekananda*. 2 vols. Calcutta: Advaita Ashrama, 1979–1981.

Isherwood, Christopher. *Ramakrishna and His Disciples*. New York: Simon and Schuster, 1965.

Nikhilananda, Swami, trans. *The Gospel of Sri Ramakrishna*. New York: Ramakrishna-Vivekananda Center, 1953.

———, ed. *Jnana Yoga*. New York: Ramakrishna-Vivekananda Center, 1955.

———, ed. *Karma Yoga and Bhakti Yoga*. New York: Ramakrishna-Vivekananda Center, 1955.

————, ed. *Raja Yoga*. New York: Ramakrishna-Vivekananda Center, 1956.

————. *Vivekananda: A Biography*. New York: Ramakrishna-Vivekananda Center, 1953.

————, ed. *Vivekananda: The Yogas and Other Works*. New York: Ramakrishna-Vivekananda Center, 1956.

Prabhavananda, Swami, trans. *How to Know God: The Yoga Aphorisms of Patanjali*. Hollywood: Vedanta Press, 1966.

————, trans. *Narada's Way of Divine Love*. Hollywood: Vedanta Press, 1971.

————. *The Spiritual Heritage of India*. Hollywood: Vedanta Press, 1963.

Prabhavananda, Swami, and Frederick Manchester, trans. *The Upanishads*. Hollywood: Vedanta Press, 1947.

Radhakrishnan, S., trans. *The Bhagavad Gita*. London: George Allen & Unwin, 1948.

————. *Indian Philosophy*. 2 vols. New York: Macmillan, 1923–1927.

Rolland, Romain. *The Life of Vivekananda and the Universal Gospel*. Calcutta: Advaita Ashrama, 1979.

Smith, Huston. *The World's Religions*. San Francisco: HarperSanFrancisco, 1991.

Vivekananda, Swami. *The Complete Works of Swami Vivekananda*. 8 vols. Calcutta: Advaita Ashrama, 1962.

ABOUT THE EDITOR

Dave DeLuca has been a professional seminar leader and speaker for over twenty years. A longtime student of the wisdom of ancient India at the Vedanta Society of Southern California, he has been one of the West's most passionate and highly regarded Vedanta teachers for over a decade. He has presented services, classes, and workshops on spiritual growth at Vedanta temples, churches, conferences, and learning centers all over the United States, and in 2004 he spoke on the origins of yoga study in the West at the Parliament of the World's Religions in Barcelona, Spain. He was initiated by Swami Swahananda, senior monk of the venerated Ramakrishna Order of India, whose guru was a direct disciple of Sri Ramakrishna. Dave's first book, *Pathways to Joy*, is a compilation of the yoga teachings of Swami Vivekananda.

To learn more about Dave, please visit www.davedeluca.com. If you would like to have Dave speak or present one of his seminars to your group, please contact him at dave@davedeluca.com.